Modern house

Phaidon Press Limited
Regent's Wharf
All Saints Street
London N1 9PA

First published 1995
Reprinted 1995, 1996
© 1995 Phaidon Press Limited
ISBN 0 7148 2889 0

A CIP catalogue record for this book is available from the British Library

Printed in Hong Kong

Captions
Page 3: Tadao Ando, Kidosaki house, Setagaya, Tokyo, 1982–86.
Page 4: Masaharu Takasaki, Zero Cosmology, Kagoshima, Kyushu, 1989–91.

John Welsh

Modern house

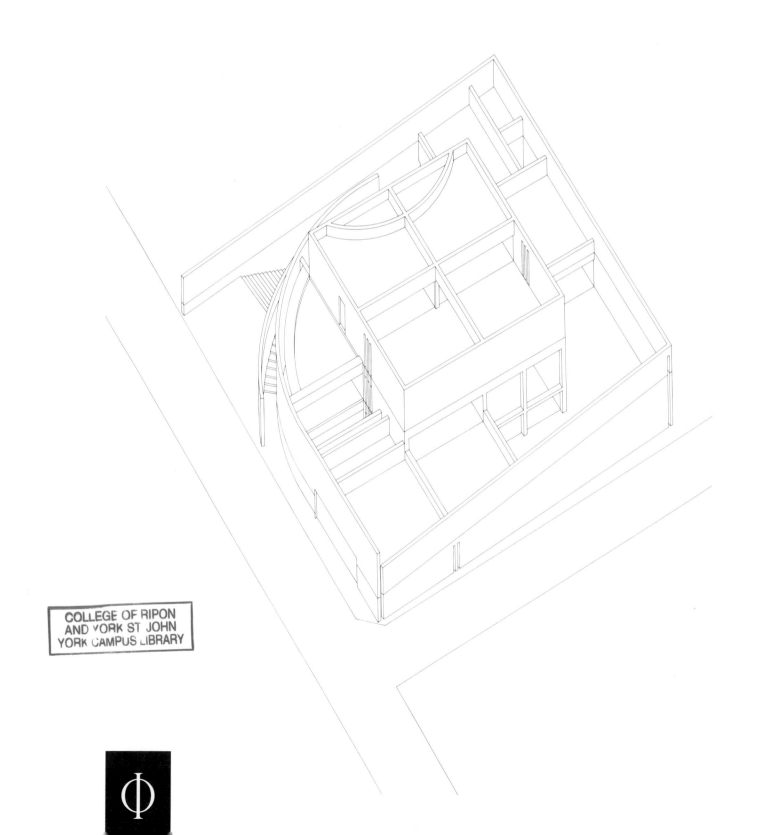

Φ

Contents

Introduction

Modern house

Charles and Ray Eames, Eames House, Pacific Palisades, California, 1949.

Over the last decade architecture has entered the international media system: now we see buildings, no less than earthquakes, political coups or celebrity weddings, projected as images rapidly round the globe. The result has been the condensation of what formerly took years; a radical new design or a slight shift in style scarcely lasts a moment before its novelty or subtlety becomes common currency.

It is difficult to imagine, therefore, the impact of F.R.S. Yorke's *The Modern House* (1934) on the sedate architectural world of 1930s Britain. Arts and crafts, art nouveau and art deco had all offered, in their turn, an alternative to the dominating Gothic revivalism of the late nineteenth century. But each was either dead or dying. Yorke, instead, filled his book with a revolutionary image; small, private villas in the modernist manner.

The shock was all the greater in Britain in its traditional isolation from mainland Europe. On the continent, modernist buildings were part of a larger cultural movement already more than a generation old, which included experiments in painting and writing, such as cubism, surrealism and Dadaism. Le Corbusier, for example, could build, publish books, edit magazines and paint impressively, all for an audience way beyond the confines of the French architectural profession. Britain, meanwhile, had to wait until 1936, for example, before the first surrealist exhibition was staged. Yorke was in a prime position both to observe developments on the continent and to bring them to a wide, British audience.

Yorke (1906–62) belonged to a small, exclusive circle of largely *émigré* architects. This group included Wells Coates, a Canadian, Berthold Lubetkin, a Russian, and Ove Arup, who founded the MARS group in 1933. Their mission was the introduction of continental modernism to Britain, either through the medium of their own work, or through publication. Yorke had completed reinforced-concrete houses at Gidea Park, Essex, in 1933 and went on to work with the Hungarian Marcel Breuer between 1935 and 1937.

Such relationships exposed Yorke to developments on the continent before many of his contemporaries. They also provided him with the sort of contacts necessary to encourage overseas architects to send him drawings and details of their work for publication. Sixty years later a book on houses completed within the past ten years can present no such radical break with its recent past. First, the speed with which ideas criss-cross the world has left few developments unexposed. Second, modernism is now rather *unmodern* in the sense that it is no longer new and provides the architect with 60 to 70 years of historical examples. This book, therefore, is not a record of change, like Yorke's book, but, rather, a record of continuity.

Novelty or mere pastiche aside, the two eras are, however, comparable for other reasons. Yorke's book was partly the result of his useful contacts, but it also reflected the architectural landscape after a short, but undoubtedly inspirational, boom in building. The world economy of the mid-1930s was no great powerhouse for the future, but there had been enough stock-market peaks and manufacturing successes in the preceding ten years to produce a new class of wealthy clients.

The entrepreneur is a familiar character throughout history but the late 1920s and early 1930s saw the arrival of the first business class in the modern era. Some of these new men were no different from their counterparts before the first world war, aspiring to the trappings of the antique aristocracy. But others had greater confidence in their worth, and were proud of a new technical age where the car and vacuum cleaner had replaced the requirement for a huge stable or costly household. The modern villa, with its streamlined appearance and efficient interior, was well-suited to such interests.

Yorke's book, therefore, is a witness to something approaching a historical coincidence. Modernism's foremost exponents, such as Mies van der Rohe and Le Corbusier, operated in European countries whose rollercoaster economies could throw up occasional millionaires as easily as they could mass unemployment. These clients, who

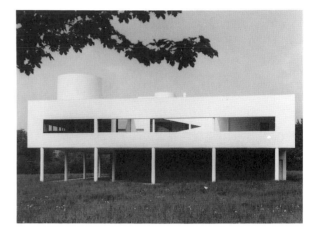

Mies van der Rohe,
Tugendhat house,
Brno, 1930 (left).
Le Corbusier, Villa Savoye,
Poissy, 1929-31 (right).

neither belonged to, nor were welcomed by, the aristocracy, reasoned that if the new rich could not join the aristocracy, they could at least beat them. What better way to do that than through fashion?

Modernism, on the rise, was the perfect vehicle. The crisp white walls of Le Corbusier's Villa Savoye or the all-glass garden façade of Mies' Tugendhat house made a clear statement about a manufacturer's wealth. What the client failed to acquire through the *soi-disant* legitimacy of a historic palazzo or villa, the client made up for by being on the cutting-edge of the modish new taste. The style was also safe, for, however radical the technology required to achieve the buildings, however experimental the organizational ideas, on the domestic front Le Corbusier and Mies were scarcely social revolutionaries. Such an interpretation of early modernism as the pursuit of the fashionable rather than a politically motivated tool would appear cynical. But the perception of modernism has remained far from unchanged over the past 60 years.

CIAM (Congrès Internationaux d'Architecture Moderne), a series of international architectural conferences held between 1928 and 1956, was an attempt by some of Europe's leading modernists to 'drag architecture from the academic impasse and place it in its proper social and economic milieu'. The bold, and sometimes hopelessly optimistic, declarations of the congresses sought to define the

responsibility of the architect. Most notable was the Athens Charter, the result of CIAM IV in 1933. Modern architecture was perceived as the pursuit of town planning, where cities were to be zoned according to function and people housed in tower blocks separated by green belts. It is telling that the event took place on a cruise ship between Marseilles and Athens.

It was only after the second world war that modernism was turned from a mere style or ideology into buildings on a vast scale. Western Europe's new welfare states saw modernism as a quick, cheap and hygienic means to accommodate their peoples whilst evoking a suitable sense of post-war pride, while Eastern Europe's totalitarian regimes pounced on modernism as the appropriately anonymous style for the proletariat. Modernism consequently became a common and increasingly devalued architectural currency.

In the 1940s and 1950s building types were repeated *en masse* and with little sophistication. Mass housing predominated at a scale very different from the niceties of the small, private villa of the 1930s. Early modernism, which had been the product of the intellectual avant-garde, became the middle-aged modernism of the corporate state. As such, it no longer represented the élite but the masses, making it totally unsuitable for the aspirations of the newly wealthy. The tastes of post-war entrepreneurs once again

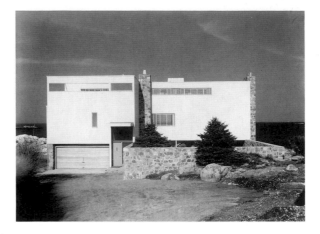

Pierre Koenig, Case Study
House #22, Hollywood,
California, 1960.

coincided with those of the European aristocracy; distinction could be assumed once more by acquiring the trappings of gentility.

Modernism ran to quite a different timetable in the United States, where conversion to the new ideas had been somewhat delayed. London, in the 1930s, was the first stop for many architects fleeing the rise of Nazism in Germany. Some arrived and settled, like Yorke's later partner Eugene Rosenberg. Others, like Walter Gropius, only ever saw Britain as a temporary stop-over on the way to the promised glories and generous salaries of America. Gropius, for example, who arrived in Britain in 1934 to work with Maxwell Fry, left to teach at Harvard University in 1937. With Gropius and others, such as Marcel Breuer, went the modernist private villa, arriving and succeeding in the US as if the great wave that had swept across Europe in the 1920s and 1930s, leaving a trough behind it in the 1940s and 1950s, had now crossed the Atlantic.

In the US, the small, modernist villa became and has remained the preserve of the rich; immune from and untainted by either the repetitiveness of social housing or the narrow-mindedness of suburban tract housing. Proof of both the American lack of social commitment and the conservatism of its middle classes rests with the results of the Case Study House programme (pages 76–77). A plan to provide affordable modern housing types for low and middle income Californians, it was organized by a local architectural magazine, but did nothing of the sort; American society had no means to provide housing, and most Los Angelenos preferred tract bungalows. Rich Californians, though, got a brand-new style through which to express their lifestyles. Yorke's book reflects the American experience; later, post-war editions of *The Modern House* were filled increasingly with houses from the United States.

Today, some parallels can be drawn between attitudes to modernism from both clients and architects, in the 1930s and the 1990s. Architecture has seen a strong return to the small, private villa around the world. Many have been created by anonymous architects. But, more importantly for this book, many architects who saw public buildings, such as art galleries and museums, as the real test of their skill in the 1960s and 1970s, have suddenly taken up the villa as a worthy vehicle for their skills. Now, the private house, with the right sort of client, can offer a level of experimentation and improvisation to rival the most high-profile university or office building. The right kind of clients have also begun to reappear, their renewed interest a result of new money, just like the 1930s.

The boomtime economies of 1980s north America, Britain and Australia produced the same sort of people as did the 1920s and 1930s. Assorted presidents and prime ministers, such as Ronald

F.R.S. Yorke, house at
Hatfield, 1935 (opposite,
above). Maxwell Fry, Sun
House, Hampstead, London,
1935 (opposite, below).
Berthold Lubetkin, house at
Whipsnade, 1937.

Reagan, Brian Mulroney, Margaret Thatcher and
Bob Hawke, slashed taxes for the better-off, creating
a new class of rich. Few were philanthropists; the
1980s had turned selfishness into a political
mantra, preaching either that 'society' did not
exist, or that their own gains were simply a matter
of personal effort, available to all those who
worked hard. These were entrepreneurs, not
particularly interested in aping the cultural mores
of earlier eras.

The exception to this global rule was Britain.
The establishment, despite the unpopularity of
social housing, was more than ready for decent
modern architects to continue to build the
nation's airports, galleries or schools, but never its
houses. The new rich were still humiliatingly
enmeshed in the confusion of class. When money
was made, it was spent on acquiring exquisite
historic manor houses in a vain attempt to join
some long-gone aristocracy like, for example, the
performance of Cypriot millionaire Asil Nadir.
Britain can, therefore, boast of its architects
designing houses overseas, but there are few of
worth in this country. Those that do exist are built
largely by and for architects.

The US and Australia have demonstrated a
different attitude: there a house was not some first-
generation, ancestral home, but rather an
immediate statement of success and taste; simply
one part of a wider portfolio of possessions. And

just as the rich started to buy paintings, such as
easy-on-the-eye impressionists, because of the
name, so they began to see their house as yet
another label-laden possession. 'I've got my Renoir',
you could imagine them saying, 'and now I'm
going to have a Gehry.'

In the US, the desire to preserve one's name in
domestic brick has a history as long as the century.
One rich example is the relationship between
Frank Lloyd Wright and the Larkin company of
Buffalo. At the turn of the century, the mail order
company was at the height of its financial success,
nominally run by the patriarch and founder John
Larkin but increasingly by two brothers Darwin D.
and W. E. Martin. So impressed was the younger
generation with Wright that the architect
ultimately constructed nine different buildings for
the company; the famous headquarters building
but also a number of luxurious homes for the
Martins, their family and fellow directors.

Here was an American company acquiring a
corporate identity through the time-honoured
route of architectural excellence, no different from
the post-war Seagram buildings of Mies van der
Rohe or more recent Siemens style by Richard
Meier. The Martins took it further, though, turning
their corporate affairs into a scaled-up version of
their own domestic arrangements. Wright's
patrons were not usually so complex (until the
later relationship with the Price family [see page

151]), seeking out Wright as a famous, fashionable name. The architectural house, therefore, has a long, unbroken genealogy in the US, so much so that tradition dictates the reverse for American entrepreneurs in comparison with British ones; a new building rather than an old one.

In Australia, the house has taken on far greater symbolic value. For too long the history of Australia has followed the development of its cities rather than the birth of a national identity. The city, meanwhile, has taken a route closer to an American model: little interest in the *civitas* of shared monuments or public spaces; buildings following the parameters set by developers rather than aesthetics; and the growth of massive, scarcely planned suburbs unconnected to any public transport.

Indeed, the Australian suburb is as dull as any American equivalent, though worse for its confused identity. The US can, at least, boast of an 'American' suburb, characterized by its tract housing and zoning. The Australian model can only offer suburbs replicating in detail English garden-city ideals and forms transplanted from the other side of the globe.

The appearance of the modernist villa in Australia, therefore, is indicative of not so much a new entrepreneurial class – many of the Australian houses in this book are by and for architects, like those in Britain – as an increasing sense of national identity, often expressed through architecture. The beauty of a home by Glenn Murcutt (page 225) or Nonda Katsalidis (page 170), for example, is rooted in the same patriotic psyche as the Sydney Opera House, but rendered on a somewhat smaller and domestic scale.

Continental Europe offers as much variety again, each nationality and social system creating a suitable group of clients. The socialist governments of France, under president François Mitterrand and Spain, under prime minister Felipe Gonzalez, initiated huge building programmes. Mitterrand sought to grace the French capital with major cultural buildings, a goal imitated rather badly by too many provincial French mayors. The Spanish had rather more modest ambitions, seeking to improve the infrastructure of Barcelona for the 1992 Olympics and Seville for Expo '92.

Similar regimes did not produce similar results. The president might well have commissioned Jean-Michel Wilmotte to design some of the domestic quarters of the Elysée palace, but a vast public programme of patronage did not go beyond public buildings to educate a new class of domestic clients. In Spain, however, the modernist villa has become a further expression of post-Franco creativity.

Northern Europe is equally confusing. The Dutch can boast of an entire nation housed in modernist buildings, but a welfare state that

Glenn Murcutt, Laurie Short house, Terrey Hills, New South Wales, 1972-73.

decently accommodates the majority has taxed a large base of rich clients out of existence. Belgium, with more than 80 per cent of the population in private homes, is quite the reverse. The modern villa is not the goal of the idle rich but often that of the moderately wealthy.

What draws all these countries together, however, is their approach to modernism. An architect offers efficiency, novelty and label value. Whether that comes as a post-modern folly, a neo-classical house or a modernist villa is largely irrelevant. The majority of clients seek an advertisement of their own wealth or satisfaction of their own personal whim. They are rarely in the business of either fighting the battles of architects or being martyrs for an entire architectural movement.

The villas in this book, therefore, represent modernism as just one style among and equal to many. The architect might see modernism as the only rational route for construction but, to the client, the crisp lines of a neo-Corb house or the transparency of a neo-Mies glass-and-steel pavilion represent little more than a choice akin to selecting a painting from a Sotheby's catalogue. It is this attitude, so similar to that of the 1930s, that links this book, once more, back to Yorke. That modernism, rather than art deco or neo-classicism, for example, still dominates the private villa, confirms not the efficiency of modernism, but its

visual power to fulfil the aspirations of a certain type of client.

That it does should come as little surprise. The 30 or so houses in this book, refreshing as they are, are far from original inventions. Instead, each one can be linked back to five or six seminal modern houses – note the similarities between the house by Stéphane Beel and Marcel Breuer's of 1947 (page 79) or the house by Pawson and Silvestrin and the work of Luis Barragán (page 33). The contemporary examples are clever in their response to brief and location but their success also rests with their ability to translate a fixed set of images, often merely photographic, from one era to another.

Yorke could not make the same kind of links. First, he genuinely believed modernism to be a radical new departure. Second, no analytical methods had been invented with which to deal with modernism. The two together obscured a lineage for modern houses that was only just becoming clear, forcing Yorke to overlook what is now the evident link between, for example, the scale and proportions of early Le Corbusier or Mies and the work of some nineteenth-century architects. What this book can do, that Yorke's did not, is to make explicit that historic link. For Yorke, though in a fortunate position to observe the arrival of modernism, was confronted with a dilemma.

The Modern House was far from parochial, boasting houses by Le Corbusier, Erich Mendelsohn and

Marcel Breuer, house, New Canaan, Connecticut, 1947.

many other modernist architects from across France, the Netherlands and Germany. By 1937, Yorke could publish a second book, *The Modern House in England*, witness to the remarkably sudden arrival of modernism in Britain. Many of the houses were by some of those early *émigrés*, such as Berthold Lubetkin and Marcel Breuer, but others were by some of Britain's homegrown talent, such as Maxwell Fry and Denys Lasdun.

Yorke's problem, though, was one of nomenclature. The earlier book divides up houses by countries. The later book resorts to 'concrete', 'frame' and 'brick', relying only on the method of construction to differentiate between buildings. Such simplistic terms were well within the reasoning of the time. The new architecture was supposed to be the result of advances in building technology. Yorke's labels were, therefore, a logical response to such developments, guiding the reader through the unknown.

But another analytical method for just these sorts of buildings was about to revolutionize architectural theory. Sir Nikolaus Pevsner's *Pioneers of Modern Design*, published in 1936, showed that the new architecture was the logical outcome of developments not only in the techniques of construction, but also in the aesthetic pursuits of late nineteenth-century architects and designers. The proposition gave the new architecture a historical legitimacy that was as valid as the

architecture of any earlier era. The book also forced all later twentieth-century architectural critics and historians to acknowledge that the modern movement was not some isolated event, but a movement with clear and explicable roots.

Yorke's books were published too early to participate in the creation of Pevsnerian links. Today, such placing is standard. But the intervening period creates one further dimension; the houses in this book can be linked not simply to pre-modern movement buildings, but also through the rich products of the past 60 years. Contemporary houses, therefore, need not be differentiated simply by their construction or nineteenth-century roots, but, rather, through a typology of historical example.

The houses in this book are, therefore, broken down into four sections, each one relating to historical models of the early modern period. Thus 'The model villa' takes Le Corbusier's Villa Savoye (1929–31) as an ideal of the house as object placed uncompromisingly in the landscape. The chapter on 'Structural solutions' takes Mies' Farnsworth house (1946–50) as the exemplar of an architecture where the exploration of structure generates the aesthetic.

The 'Organic house' makes reference to Frank Lloyd Wright, both to his more contextual work, such as Fallingwater (1935–39), and his more decorative or zoomorphic proclivities, such as

**Norman Foster & Partners,
vacation house, Corsica, 1993.**

those developed by his student Bruce Goff. Finally, the 'Urban compromise' explores houses where the city or suburb has compromised an architectural principle but in the process enhanced the original idea: Pierre Chareau's Maison de Verre (1928–31), for example, or Le Corbusier's Maisons La Roche–Jeanneret (1923-25). This methodology, however, confronts to some extent the architectural diversity of the post-modern era.

The immediate followers of Le Corbusier, Mies or Wright took their masters' work to different types and scales of buildings but kept rigidly to form. The immediate post-war work of American architects Skidmore Owings & Merrill – New York's Lever House (1952), for example – can be seen as a direct reference to Mies' work. But the past two decades have seen a far less dogmatic approach, so that an architect such as Sir Norman Foster can make reference to Miesian formality in the Nîmes Carré d'Art (1993), but resort to the pragmatism of Charles Eames or another of the Case Study House architects in the design of the more recent vacation house on Corsica built for the mayor of that town.

This book reflects that destruction of the modernist primacy, accepting a far greater diversity of inspiration. The coloured abstract walls, the gushing waterspouts, the intrusion of local stone, all are features used by modernist architects who find Luis Barragán's work far more sympathetic than the uncompromising position of Le Corbusier. Some architects, seeking the perfection of a Miesian pavilion, need to express more than merely formality and rigidity. Charles and Ray Eames' own house at Pacific Palisades, in California, Case Study House #8 (1949), shows a means to accommodate the paraphernalia, both physical and spiritual, of the modern world. And Pevsner provides the means to resolve such formal confusion. For *Pioneers of Modern Design* also empowered future architectural critics, allowing them, not the architects, to resolve the proper placing and analysis of their work. So Xaveer de Geyter might see himself as an architect exploring structurally expressive architecture. Yorke, for example, would have placed him in his chapter on 'Frame'. But the villa at Brasschaat (see page 162) is, in reality, a wilful exploitation of context, placing it among the better organic houses of the late twentieth century. And so it goes on, until only a very few architects such as Alberto Campo Baeza or OMA could claim to stick firmly to only one inspirational model. The contemporary legitimacy of architectural diversity is not reflected in the contemporary critics' role. They have, through Pevsner, more history, more models and more time with which to define.

But the final definition of this book is as a snapshot in time. F.R.S. Yorke's *The Modern House* is a record of a creative, though sadly short, era of architecture, when the economic, social and aesthetic factors of pre-second-world-war society converged to create some of the twentieth century's most impressive modern masterpieces. This book, 60 years later, is no less of an 'Instamatic' image, preserving the products of a politically and spiritually selfish though equally creative, decade. What has changed, however, is the nature of modernism. Whether for private or public buildings, modernism has remained the principal architectural idiom throughout the intervening period, forcing this book to be not a record of change, but a polemic of continuity.

Pevsner, Nikolaus. *Pioneers of Modern Design.* London: Architectural Press, 1936.
Yorke, F.R.S. *The Modern House.* London: Architectural Press, 1934.
Yorke, F.R.S. *The Modern House in England.* London: Architectural Press, 1937.

Chapter 1

The model villa

Luis Barragán, Las Arboledas, Mexico City, 1958-61 (left).
Glenn Murcutt, Magney House, Kempsey, New South Wales, 1988-90 (below).

If all contemporary houses make reference to a historical model, then the clearest example of the endurance of such ideas must be those houses that look for inspiration to the model villa. Take, for example, Le Corbusier's Villa Savoye (1929–31), rising on its *pilotis* above an uncut meadow in suburban Poissy. The purity of such a building has produced the clearest definition of the strand of modernism that sees architecture not as a collage of decoration and materials but as a distillation of all domestic functions into an abstract form. The Villa Savoye, therefore, is placed as an object in the landscape. Context is uncompromisingly neglected, but Le Corbusier creates a precise, geometric whole.

Our post-war era has, however, legitimized architecture – liberating it, perhaps – as a process of 'pick 'n' mix'. One dogmatic modernist style, such as Le Corbusier's rationalism now often runs parallel to a more pragmatic, equally respected expression of similarly abstract goals. So, the uncompromising nature of the model villa has encouraged an alternative dialogue. Some architects have looked not to the work of Le Corbusier, but to the work of others such as Luis Barragán, finding in his houses, scattered throughout Mexico, a similar quality of abstraction, but one more firmly rooted in its location through the use of colour or local materials.

The roots of Le Corbusier's rigid vision have been explained clearly by Colin Rowe.[1] He makes explicit the link between Le Corbusier's work and classical architecture; both sought not an idealization of their surroundings but to be the ideal in their surroundings. Rowe compares Andrea Palladio's Villa Rotonda (Villa Almerico-Capra), near Vicenza (finally finished by 1569),[2] to Le Corbusier's Villa Savoye, Poissy (1929–31); both Rotonda and Savoye are viewed in the round, each rising from what Rowe interprets as a 'Virgilian' landscape. He elaborates this argument with the Villa Foscari at Mira (1560) and the Villa Stein at Garches (1927). Palladio's bucolic ideals were replaced, however, by Le Corbusier's interest in the contemporary world of technology; 'if the architecture at the Rotonda forms the setting for the good life, at Poissy it is certainly the background for a lyrically efficient one,' says Rowe.[3]

This premise, despite its drawbacks, has been sufficient for many architects. Richard Meier's houses are influenced by Le Corbusier, but Meier (see page 36) takes his interest beyond mere references to Corbusian forms. Le Corbusier pushed his fascination with contemporary technology to the limit; Meier takes up where his predecessor left off, exploiting the potential of today's materials to the full. Alberto Campo Baeza turns to a more metaphysical interpretation of Le Corbusier's work, placing simple, one-storey houses within the Spanish countryside (see page 56). The contrast between the lush surroundings and the white block is welcome, the resulting abstraction being a key goal of Campo Baeza's work.

Tadao Ando (see page 65) willingly admits to the influence of Le Corbusier's 'five points' from the 1920s. The rich variety of interior and exterior spaces, independent of location, of Le Corbusier's villas suggests solutions to the claustrophobic nature of the Japanese urban experience. Ando's houses cut themselves off from this maelstrom, creating another world around a private courtyard. (Comparisons abound with the suggestions of blissful existence on the balconies of the freehold maisonettes in Le Corbusier's drawings.)

But Ando's pursuit of Corbusian aesthetics, rather than technique, can also be seen as the enrichment of modern architecture with references to the traditional Japanese building. Le Corbusier's and Ando's smooth planes and easy access to outdoor spaces could easily be seen as the twentieth-century, concrete equivalent of the historic Japanese house with its movable screens. Le Corbusier constantly returns to the importance of light in his writings; Ando is no less keen, but sees the nature of light and its transformation of an interior as particular to the Japanese character.

Le Corbusier's work, however, which, in his own words from *Vers une architecture*, provides the 'mass-production house, healthy (and morally so too) and beautiful in the same way that the working tools and instruments that accompany our

existence are beautiful', might have been poetry when built by Le Corbusier but is too difficult for later, less talented architects. Rowe sees the problem as, 'in the case of derivative works, it is perhaps an adherence to "rules" which has lapsed'. The desire for a more human masonry form is illustrated in E. T. A. Hoffmann's tale of Councillor Krespel from 1818, as retold by Anthony Vidler in *The Architectural Uncanny*.

A wealthy German townsman has a house built at the end of his garden, without the help of drawings or an architect. Workmen, instead, raise the walls without any openings from four square foundations until Krespel orders a halt. The councillor, pacing up and down his garden, then orders a door to be cut out and indicates where windows should be formed from the interior. Krespel's daughter, Antonia, caught within the house, finally dies. Vidler sees this fable as evidence of the inhumanity of houses built to such rationalism.

Even Le Corbusier's contemporaries were struggling against the frigidity of the new modernism. Tristan Tzara argued that 'modern architecture, as hygienic and stripped of ornaments as it wants to appear, has no chance of living', proposing, instead, an 'intrauterine' architecture of shelter.[5] The Dadaist poet's solution was a house in Paris by Adolf Loos (1926) which sought privacy through a massive masonry façade.

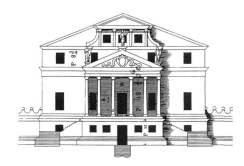

Andrea Palladio, Villa Foscari,
Mira, 1560 (above, right).
Le Corbusier, Villa Savoye,
Poissy, 1929-31 (below).

Le Corbusier, Villa Stein,
Garches, Paris, 1927.

Luis Barragán, San Cristobal stable, pool and house, Los Clubes, Mexico City, 1967-68 (left). Luis Barragán, Antonio Galvez house, San Angel, Mexico City, 1955 (below).

Vidler takes the debate through to today, discussing Le Corbusier in the language of post-Freudian analysis: 'If houses were no longer haunted by the weight of tradition and the evidence of generations of family drama, if no cranny was left for storage of the bric-à-brac once deposited in damp cellars and musty attics, then memory would be released from its unhealthy preoccupations to live in the present'.[6]

Goodbye, Le Corbusier, hello, Luis Barragán: 'My house is my refuge, an emotional piece of architecture, not a cold piece of convenience.'[7] While Le Corbusier looked to the past grandeur of Rome, Barragán sought inspiration from cultures closer to home. His earliest memories were of a village called Mazamitla, where water was carried 5 metres above the roofs of houses in gutted logs, the water descending into fountains in a private patio.[8] Barragán's own architecture, however, moved through three stages before he achieved a comfortable compromise.

His early work, in his home town of Guadalajara (1927–36), was heavily influenced by Moorish architecture. Then Barragán moved to Mexico City, where he designed private houses and apartment blocks with references to the work of Le Corbusier. A two-family house on the Avenida Parque (1936), for example, has a strip of continuous, horizontal windows on the top storey. Concrete frames, or *brise-soleils*, sit on top of the roof, framing the views

of the city from the roof garden; both features appearing, for example, on Le Corbusier's double-family house for Stuttgart's Weißenhofsiedlung (1927).

Barragán's purchase of the volcanic acres at El Pedegral in 1945 and his design of both landscape features and zoning code for modern houses were the last phase and first signs of his own contribution to modern architecture. The fantastic shapes of nature were left in place but any human intervention, either house or landscape feature, was a series of horizontal or vertical planes set into the landscape. The insertions achieved a level of empathy with their surroundings through the use of local materials rather than the ubiquitous white render, and through Barragán's poetic composition. His architecture acquired a level of abstraction as skilful as any artist could have achieved.

The result was Barragán's series of post-war houses. His own house at Tacubaya (1947) 'owes little to the international style of modern architecture. It represents a most subtle elaboration of that part of Mexico's provincial architecture Barragán loved so much; its ranches, villages, convents'.[9] The roof terrace started as a partially walled enclosure open to the garden, but, with time, Barragán filled in the fourth side and painted one wall red and one brown. But it was the stable, horse pool, swimming pool and house for Mr and Mrs Folke Egerstrom at Los Clubes (1967–68) where the pink walls, water pools and spouts came together to create what Emilio Ambasz

Adolf Loos, house for Tristan Tzara, Paris, 1926.

considers 'a lyric effortlessness, two aspects of high ritual; the suggestion of a space beyond and even one magically transubstantiated'.[10]

For many architects, these explanations ground their work in a far firmer historical and social base. Antoine Predock (see page 49), for example, working in New Mexico/Arizona, was confronted with a Spanish/Pueblo architectural tradition that had encouraged vulgar, historicist buildings in adobe.[11] Barragán provides a way out, legitimizing the use of local materials but showing that the massive forms of adobe architecture could be recreated as the almost brutalist forms of Predock's design.

The link is even more evident in a house by Pawson and Silvestrin (see page 33). The architects' previous work was largely city-centre apartments, where every normal element of home was reduced to the barest of essentials. Their client, though, wanted a Spanish-style hacienda. The final result, the Neuendorf house, is not much of a compromise with its massive, largely blind, enclosing walls.

Pawson and Silvestrin have, however, turned to Barragánesque features to create an architecture that is firmly rooted in its surroundings. Local soil, for example, has been mixed with cement to render the walls. The entrance atrium, open to the sky though surrounded by four walls, could be Barragán's own roof garden. And the water rushing from a spout at the end of the pool recalls Barragán's village of Mazamitla.

In one way, the Neuendorf house achieves the sort of formal composition Le Corbusier might have sought, but it also meets the needs of a different generation of architects to achieve an architecture more responsive to place and less obsessed with a machine-oriented perfection.

1. Rowe, Colin. *The mathematics of the ideal villa and other essays.* Cambridge, MA: MIT Press, 1988.
2. Fletcher, Sir Banister. *A History of Architecture*, 19th edn. London: Butterworth, 1987. All references to the Rotonda are taken from this edition.
3. Rowe, Colin (see footnote 1).
4. Vidler, Anthony. *The Architectural Uncanny*. Cambridge, MA: MIT Press, 1992.
5. Tzara, Tristan. 'D'un certain automatisme du Goût', *Minotaure*, 3–4 December 1933, trans. Anthony Vidler.
6. Vidler, Anthony (see footnote 4).
7. Ambasz, Emilio. *The architecture of Luis Barragán*. New York: MOMA, 1976.
8. Ibid.
9. Ibid.
10. Ibid.
11. Mead, Christopher. *Houses by Bart Prince*. Albuquerque: University of New Mexico Press, 1991.

John Pawson/ Claudio Silvestrin
Neuendorf house
Mallorca, Spain, 1987–89

Architects whose work deals with the reduction of architecture to the barest possible minimum face a dilemma when confronted by the relaxed clutter of a holiday home. This is Pawson and Silvestrin's answer – a house where the entrance (below) has become a mere slit in the wall and the swimming pool and windows (opposite) have taken on the more casual forms characteristic of the Mexican architect Luis Barragán.

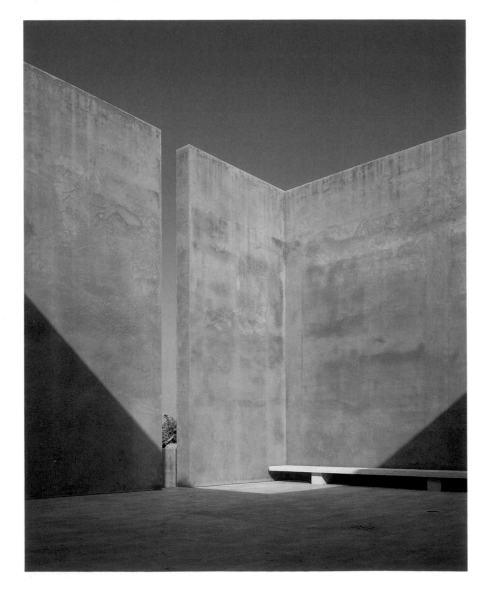

Le Corbusier's expression of houses as sculptural forms and his clever exploitation of natural light have influenced many architects. The work of John Pawson and Claudio Silvestrin, who were collaborators between 1987 and 1989, emphasizes these and one further ideal – Le Corbusier's search for minimalist reduction. The result has been a series of interiors by the architects in which everyday objects are hidden from view.

Ironically, the architects' first commission for a house does not fit so neatly into their chosen theme. The Neuendorf house is not a city apartment where clutter can be hidden away neatly in cupboards, but a holiday home for Hans Neuendorf, an art dealer, and his family, hectic with the panoply of towels and beach shoes. The architects' task, therefore, has been an act of containment to achieve anything approaching their own agenda; first of the family's natural holiday sloppiness; then of the client's original ideas, for Neuendorf's concept contrasted starkly with that of his architects.

Neuendorf, who met Pawson on holiday through a friend of a friend, took Pawson for a five-hour drive to show off a spectacular site the art dealer was assembling inland. The party went for a drink at a nearby village, where Neuendorf, rather sheepishly, produced some sketches he had made of a proposed villa. Pawson was astonished to find images for a tasteless, Spanish-style hacienda

A minimalist approach in the bathrooms of a Pawson-designed London apartment (above) and the Neuendorf house (right).

The sparse, cool interior of the Neuendorf house.

fundamentally opposed to anything in the architect's experience; how could clients, such as Neuendorf, with his exotic aesthetic proclivities, and architects, with their obsession for less than the bare essentials, ever come together?

Bruce Chatwin, after visiting one of Pawson's flats for the first time, said, 'what is not generally recognized is that "emptiness" in architecture – or empty space – is not empty, but full'. The famous travel writer remembered visiting an ex-pupil of Mies van der Rohe in his New York apartment. All his goods, including a Picasso, were hidden away in cupboards because, to him, the greatest luxury in the twentieth-century's consumerist maelstrom was freedom from a home full of possessions. 'For no matter how small the room, providing your eye could travel freely around it, the space it contained was limitless.'

Of course, such aesthetics have a long cultural history. Zen Buddhism originates with the equation of few earthly goods with greater spiritual wealth. The concept has been absorbed by Judaeo-Christian philosophy, in which poverty and simplicity have become the qualitative hallmark of everyday existence. For Chatwin, the eternal traveller of the world, such lack of baggage (physically, if not culturally) meant business. In a similar way, Neuendorf is a fellow traveller, an international businessman whose destination provides 24-hour doses of familiarity.

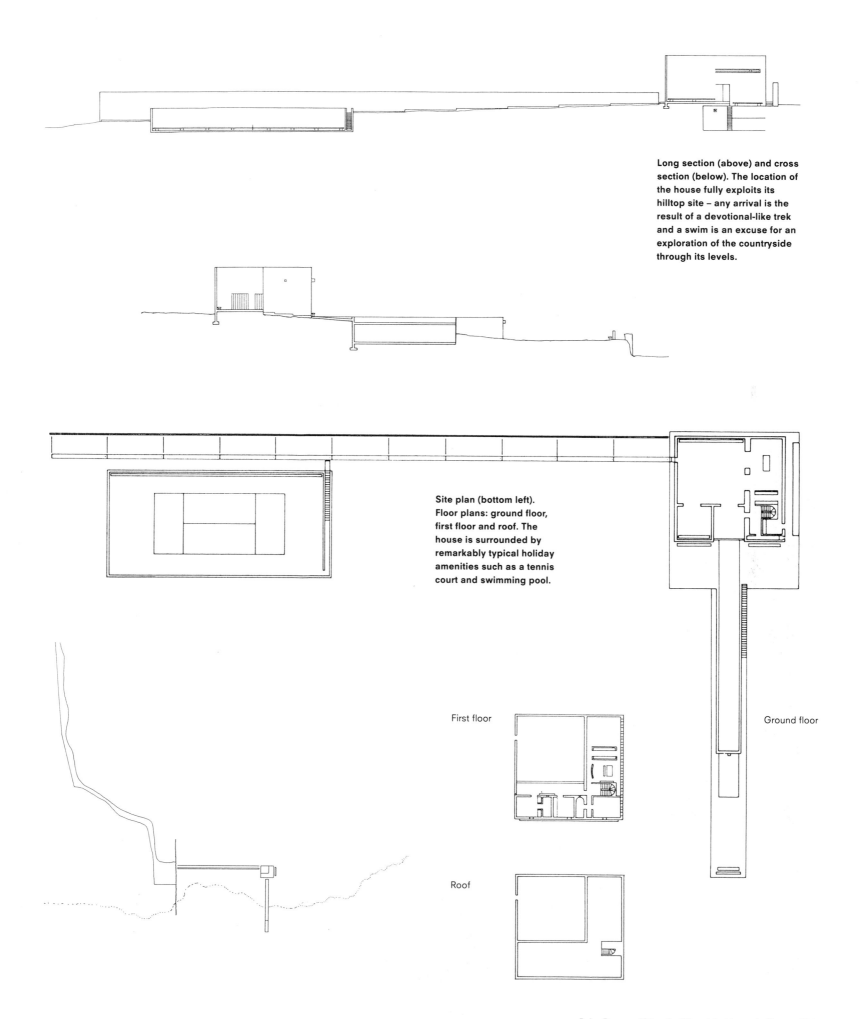

Long section (above) and cross section (below). The location of the house fully exploits its hilltop site – any arrival is the result of a devotional-like trek and a swim is an excuse for an exploration of the countryside through its levels.

Site plan (bottom left). Floor plans: ground floor, first floor and roof. The house is surrounded by remarkably typical holiday amenities such as a tennis court and swimming pool.

First floor

Roof

Ground floor

Cars are kept at a distance so that both family and friends have to approach the house up a slowly climbing flight of steps. The sense of direction is emphasized by an accompanying wall and terraces which further anchor the house within its landscape.

For Neuendorf, a simple holiday home includes exactly the kind of details that most people try desperately to avoid on holiday. An office, for example, and bedrooms for the friends/clients that make up so much of a dealer's social life. A Spanish hacienda might create momentary familiarity but little sense of repose. The solution rested with another hero of the modern movement, Luis Barragán, whose architecture, planes set into the landscape, did not look back to the myth of the machine age but forward to an abstraction of Mexico's history and ethnicity. Barragánesque features and colour created the necessary minimalism to suit the architects without neglecting the festive nature of a holiday home, and the forms themselves could be read as references to local architectural traditions.

In theory, the house is relatively straightforward. Cars are left parked at a discreet place below. The house is then approached up a flight of long, shallow steps beside a wall gradually decreasing in height, both sculpted as closely to the landscape as the entrance to Luigi Snozzi's Casa Bernasconi (see page 44). Inside, bedrooms are located at an upper level; a dining room, living room and office are on the ground floor. A long lap pool, perpendicular to those stairs, shoots out into the surrounding olive groves, its still, blue surface like the deck of an aircraft carrier ploughing through turbulent, green waves. Water from the pool then runs through a spout into an oblong pond below – just like at Barragán's mythical village of Mazamitla.

In practice, the house attains two of Pawson and Silvestrin's aesthetic objectives. Pawson admits to a weakness for walls, citing the kitchen gardens of English country houses as an ideal. Here, the entire house is a wall, rising 9 metres (29 feet, 6 inches) from the ground. The façade is as minimal as possible, blind but for a vertical slit – the entrance to the house, its width set by the dimensions of the shallow stairs – a cavernous exit to the pool and a horizontal slit for the bedroom windows. The scarcity of openings is deliberate; the architects believe that views should be framed rather than panoramic, as does Antoine Predock (see page 51), and the narrowness of the entrance makes the final entry to the house behind more dramatic still.

Neuendorf repeatedly reiterated his desire for a cool, partly shaded outdoor space, a feature common to many of the local houses. Pawson and Silvestrin re-created this in their own way with an atrium, lying behind the slit. The space is one of their London apartments transported to the summer sun, or the equivalent to the rooftop garden of Barragán's own house in Tacubaya (1947). Blank walls rise around the courtyard throwing long, cool shadows. Each of the ground-floor rooms opens on to the courtyard. Of course, such a place could become a convenient dumping ground, but

the architects have ensured otherwise. 'Furniture can ruin architecture,' says Pawson, so as much furniture as possible is fitted. Low benches, for example, are placed round the perimeter of the court – 'too many for me', says Pawson.

One feature of the Neuendorf house that stands in marked contrast to either Pawson or Silvestrin's London apartments is colour: brown rather than white. The rough, brick walls are covered in a render reddened by mixing in crushed local rock, creating an abstract object in the landscape. 'People say the house looks Moorish,' says Pawson, 'but it comes from the local architecture.' The largely unbroken surface of the walls and the colour are reminiscent of Barragán's house and stud farm for the San Cristobal estate, Mexico City (1967), a reference strengthened by the pool and waterspout. The association also links the Neuendorf house back to Pawson and Silvestrin's minimalism, for Barragán's great hero, after an early career in Mexican vernacular, was Le Corbusier.

A swimmer and a pair of beach shoes fail to break the poetry of Pawson and Silvestrin's austere architecture, proving that minimalism and holidays do go together.

From the back the Neuendorf
house seems to have been
directly inspired by a
Moorish fortress.

Richard Meier
Ackerberg house

Malibu, California, USA, 1984–86

The white railings of the Ackerberg house, so evocative of a transatlantic liner, provide a suitable theme for a seaside property. Yet, many of Richard Meier's houses, though well inland, display an identical nautical element.

Indeed, most of Meier's buildings, from private houses to museums to town halls in both the US and Europe, are designed within an extraordinarily concise architectural vocabulary. Such similarity needed little justification when Meier's workload was primarily East-Coast domestic. But can one architectural language remain equally valid for an international architect and relevant to the specific location of a Californian beach house?

Meier's constant palette of elements is not vast. Walls are often either stuccoed or covered in glass blocks or ceramic tiles. Vast, double-height panes or square holes suffice as windows. Structural cylindrical columns, railings to ramps, and *brise-soleils* add to the steamship aesthetic. Each material or form has been picked with care from the classics of the early modern movement, with Le Corbusier's Villa Savoye (1929) and Villa Stein (1927) in particular favour, and they are then reassembled as a collage. Yet, Meier's architecture does develop an identity beyond that of his predecessors, and his houses are differentiated from his public buildings.

Le Corbusier was often fortunate in the types of sites his clients offered him; generally, flat, sometimes suburban sites. But Meier has had to

Seafront façade of the Ackerberg house. Richard Meier's architectural vocabulary is a recurring exploration of geometric forms and austere materials. Yet Meier's common approach can respond to specific locations: here the laid-back, beach culture of California.

The living room walls take on two distinct Meieresque forms. One (left) curves in plan, creating one side of an intimate central courtyard, while another (opposite) forms a transition between the living room and the patio – the formality of the interior contrasting with the carefree lifestyle of the exterior.

The street façade (below), which accommodates the guest bedrooms and the garage, acts as a buffer between the constant din of passing cars and the peace and quiet of the courtyard behind.

Richard Meier, The Atheneum, New Harmony, Indiana, 1975-79 (above). Richard Meier, Douglas house, Harbor Springs, Michigan, 1973 (left).

work with more difficult situations; dramatic slopes and prominent coastlines. Every building, however superficially similar, responds to context in the best traditions of late modernism. First, Meier attempted to relate the geometry of surrounding roads to the plan as early as the Hoffman house (1967), an ambition achieved with brilliance in the Atheneum visitors' centre (1975–79). Second, each building is placed to benefit from a view and an object in the landscape. His Douglas house (1973), for example, sits high on a wooded slope above Lake Michigan, looking down on the feature of which it has become so much a part.

Technology has helped Meier to achieve such heterogeneity of form and content, whatever the condition of the site. Le Corbusier's buildings relied on materials that could not sustain the limits to which they were taken; roofs leaked because they were not sealed adequately, merely covered with asphalt which cracked. Technology has now caught up with early modernist aesthetics. Meier can build with materials that Le Corbusier could only have dreamed of. Porcelain enamel tiles, for example, clad on to frames with expansion joints in the substructure, respond to the daily changes of weather, and maintain the purity of their colour.

Such construction applies to all Meier's buildings, yet his houses have a domestic language and scale all of their own. His public buildings display a fenestration in which repetitive mullions are typical.

His houses are characterized by one huge expanse of glass, often curved, allowing views out of and into the living room. And Meier obviously tempers some of his clients' wilder fantasies. The unbuilt Rachofsky house (1985) for a wealthy Texan looks rather more like a building for Siemens than a house. Indeed, Meier states that, 'if it had been designed today, its form would be reduced in scale and would more clearly express its formal organization'.

His one-family houses allow him to keep to a set of planning rules, something that is impossible with the complicated programme of a public building. The Smith house (1965), Douglas house (1975) or the Westchester house (1986), for example, have floor plans that split the houses in two. One half contains the living/dining areas, the other the bedrooms, bathrooms and servants' quarters. The structure emphasizes this public/private divide by an open steel-and-glass frame on one side towards a view (Le Corbusier's Dom-ino), contrasting with a closed solid slab on the other side (rather more Citrohan). The true front of a house often ends up as the back, and vice versa.

The Ackerberg house breaks this rule but responds to its specific location. The coastline strip of Malibu boasts extravagant houses of little architectural value. Walls are often built right up to the property line and squeezed between the fantastic ocean and the dismal Pacific Coastal

The living room (opposite) is left intentionally sparse to accommodate the family's collection of art and provide a suitable location for entertaining on a grand scale. And yet Meier has not forgotten the necessity for intimacy within any home, as in the library (above) which is located on an open mezzanine above the living room.

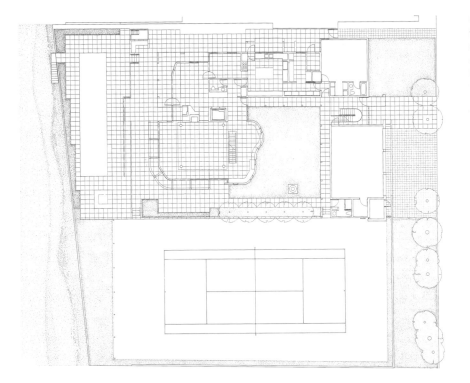

Ground floor (left) and
first floor plans (right):
a C-shaped floor plan
accommodates guests
nearest the highway,
places the living room
beside the sea and sleeps
the family in between.

Ground floor

Highway behind. The Ackerberg plot has been divided into two, with a tennis court taking up one half and a swimming pool stripped-in between house and sea. Guest bedrooms and garage lie beside the highway, insulating the house from the road. The living/dining areas are closest to the sea, with a block containing kitchen, servants' quarters and master bedroom linking the two.

Evidently Meier had to bend his rules with the Ackerberg house because, unlike his other houses, this is two wings, not one neat volume. The guest and service wings are more enclosed blocks, made private by tiles or glass bricks, while the living/dining wing is a far more open structure with more glass and fewer tiles. The C-shaped plan creates a central courtyard. The guest bedrooms are then provided with alternative views of either the highway or, more pleasantly, the courtyard, just as the link block either suffers the neighbours or enjoys the courtyard.

Meier sees the Ackerberg's court as fitting into the indigenous courtyard-style houses of southern California. The street door also opens on to the courtyard, leaving people to proceed under a loggia towards the real front door and living room beyond. The impact is phenomenal. Visitors pass through the relative peace of the lushly turfed court to enter the living room, where they are hit by a climax of sound and light off the edge of the world's biggest ocean.

That power turns the living room into a crucial zone. The square ceiling of the double-height room is supported on four cylindrical columns. The structure allows for a seamless clerestory, its purity emphasized by the absence of corner mullions, which is designed to pick up the ocean light. Walls are left white to display the family's art collection. This living room is then surrounded by space for other communal activities, arranged in a geometric plan around the square core.

The back/court wall is a double piano curve (a familiar Meier feature but this time containing a real piano). A further clerestory and single-storey curved glass windows enclose the room on two further sides. A double-height *brise-soleil* provides the room with some sun protection and privacy. It is something of a loggia as well, breaking down the division between inside and out for bathers from the pool coming into the shade.

The Ackerberg house is Malibu. Its elements embrace the Californian lifestyle with no less certainty than the houses of Neutra. There is a similar blurring between in and outdoors, with easy access from sitting room to pool, or an open air alternative to purely internal circulation. Yet, just as Neutra achieves a similarly successful synthesis of regional habits through the arrangement of his signature horizontal and vertical planes, so the very different form and materials of the Ackerberg house are unmistakably Meier.

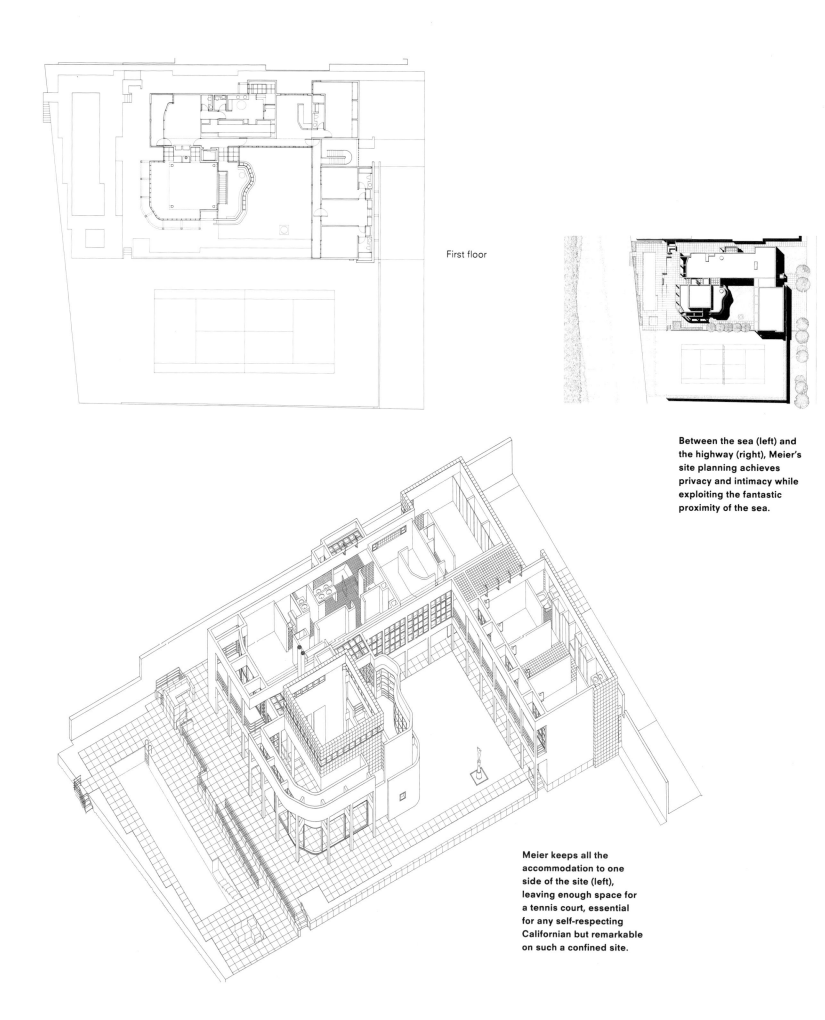

First floor

Between the sea (left) and the highway (right), Meier's site planning achieves privacy and intimacy while exploiting the fantastic proximity of the sea.

Meier keeps all the accommodation to one side of the site (left), leaving enough space for a tennis court, essential for any self-respecting Californian but remarkable on such a confined site.

Luigi Snozzi
Casa Bernasconi

Carona, Switzerland, 1988–89

'My dream at this moment', says Luigi Snozzi, 'is to build a house that is hardly seen at all, reducing everything to the indispensable.' He has done well in realizing his ambition. The Casa Bernasconi is one in a long line of neo-Corbusian houses designed by Snozzi.

Such apparent brutalism might appear to contradict Snozzi's home territory of the Ticino, repeating in the wooded valleys of Switzerland the kind of contextual mistakes perpetrated on post-war cities. But Snozzi belongs to a group of architects, the Ticinese Tendenza, who have sought to update the aesthetics of early modernism by reversing any previous disregard for the *genius loci*. But the characteristics of this architecture, so closely linked to one relatively small geographical area, must be qualified.

Marshall McLuhan's prediction of the 'global village' proved no less true for architecture than for any other contemporary activity. A building in Los Angeles or Sydney is scarcely complete before its logic or innovatory features have acquired a common visual currency in London or Tokyo. Yet, Snozzi claims to be 'just a provincial architect', belonging to what has euphemistically been called a school of 'regional' architects.

Snozzi's Ticino, the Italian-speaking canton of Switzerland, is located between the hysterical glamour of Milan to the south and the bourgeois predictability of Berne to the north. Of course,

images from elsewhere have been beamed into the area; yet, its architects appear to have been left somewhat untouched by recent architectural development towards the fantasy of deconstruction or historical revivalism. The Ticinese Tendenza have been left in peace, therefore, to concentrate on those elements of architecture that were rejected too swiftly elsewhere.

The group's strict dogma shows two strains of development. The work of a younger generation, such as Mario Botta, reflects the increasing intellectual equality granted to a variety of styles and influences in the post-modern world. Yet Botta's houses are not made to fit the site but stand as simple forms in contrast to their surroundings (see the Casa Bianda, page 161), ironic given his

The dogmatic forms of Snozzi's architecture seem at odds with a Swiss valley, yet the architect's use of solid and void, light and shade, as within the chasm-like entrance (left), sets up an abstract poetry.

The house overlooks the pool (opposite), an amenity firmly anchored to the site by its own two-storey pavilion.

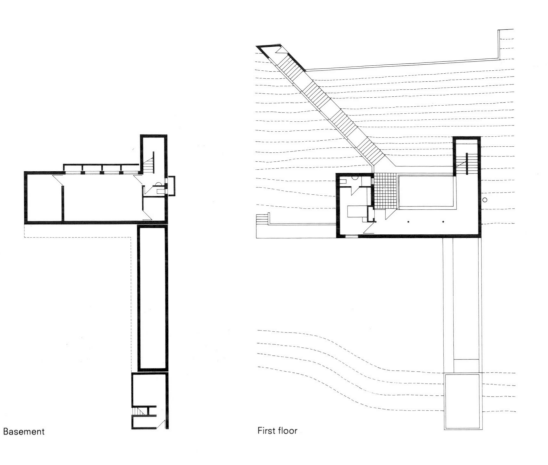

Basement

First floor

The four-storey house (in section, below) is approached from the slope above and entered on the third level, above the living room but below the bedrooms. Floor plans: basement and stores; ground floor, living room; first floor, entrance and void; second floor, bedroom.

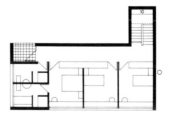

Second floor

Ground floor

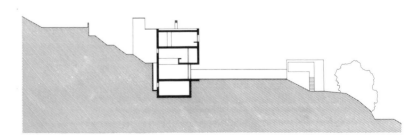

The Casa Cavalli (left) and the Casa Kalman (below).

The sitting room with the entrance level mezzanine above. The double-height volume exploits natural light, although there is little exterior expression of such volumes.

apparent lack of dogma. Snozzi, however, represents an older, stricter generation where the house as object – the standard Corbusian model – has, all the same, been refined into something smoothly contoured into the landscape.

Two early houses neatly condense Snozzi's architectural vocabulary: the Casa Cavalli (1976–78) and the Casa Kalman (1974–76). Snozzi deals with their often awkward sloping sites by linking them firmly back to the adjacent road or the street above with an *in situ* concrete ramp or sculptural staircase. Not for him the bridges of Botta, whisking people over thin air from a road to an upper-storey entrance. Snozzi obviously takes into account the often dramatic landscape. The views from the Casa Kalman are framed by frankly Corbusian *brise-soleils*. And even the more urban Casa Guidotti in Monte Carasso has an upper-storey living room with strip windows and a roof garden to take advantage of the views of the distant mountains.

Through such means, Snozzi produces powerful but far from overwhelming work. 'Every intervention becomes an art of restoration, giving shape to a design which already potentially exists,' he says. Take the Casa Bernasconi. Its layout is a very deliberate act; something Snozzi calls 'routes and limits' where a procession through the house echoes the building's footprint, emphasizing the perimeter of a home for the Bernasconis.

The entrance lies well above the house beside an approach road and parking space. Steps set diagonally to the house between two low, concrete walls then descend the hill to the portico, a deep chasm carved in the almost-blind north façade. The recessed front door opens into the heart of the house, where almost two-thirds of the interior can be seen from one spot. The bedrooms are hidden away upstairs, but a void, devouring part of the entrance-level floor, gives a view down to the living room below.

Travertine around that core encourages a conversation between two qualities of light: north, through the high-level clerestory of the portico; south, up from the sitting room. Surprisingly, the double height over the living room is not expressed by the exterior, where the fenestration does not hint at the section within. Snozzi has his reasons: the view from the living room is strictly controlled through a strip of five floor-to-ceiling windows, focusing attention on the lap pool with its loggia and the fantastic mountains beyond.

The apparently austere values of the Tendenza are now sought by architects in very different environments. Snozzi, Botta and several other members of the group, such as Livio Vacchini and Reinhart & Reichlin, have become familiar names outside the Ticino. The characteristics of a region now confront the contradiction of international fame.

Antoine Predock
Zuber house

Paradise Valley, Phoenix, Arizona, USA, 1987–89

The harsh surroundings of the Arizona desert can prove intimidating from both a practical and an aesthetic point of view. But Predock has exploited the power of the scenery and climate to produce a house at one with its location, whose interior creates a cool place of refuge for its owners.

That Antoine Predock mentions Frank Lloyd Wright as a source of inspiration is largely predictable. The Zuber house is horizontal like a Prairie house and toned to the desert like Wright's nearby Taliesin West. Predock, however, faces a dilemma. His practice in New Mexico is the inheritor of a regional architecture, one that sought to reduce the anonymity of buildings with abstract references to local materials and desert culture.

The experiment, though, has come full circle. The desert states of New Mexico and Arizona boast many buildings drawing on the Pueblo and Spanish colonial adobe buildings. In the hands of the revivalist architect John Gaw Meem, the style was mere pastiche, his Zimmerman Library at the University of New Mexico, Albuquerque (1936–39), showing little distinction from a Hollywood film set. A generation of post-war, international style architects pursued a different theme, abstracting the Spanish-Pueblo style into an earth-coloured, cubical massing of brutalism such as in the Krueger Associates' Humanities building, also for the University of New Mexico (1977). The 1980s saw the Spanish-Pueblo style re-emerge as a tool of post-modernists' historicist leanings.

Predock, who had built entirely in adobe, such as at the La Luz housing estate, Albuquerque (1970), abandoned the historicist Pueblo genre for blocks and concrete, but maintained notions of context. Predock's sensitivity to the desert states is typical of

an outsider. He was born in Missouri, studied engineering in New Mexico and qualified in architecture at New York's Columbia University. His travels on scholarship avoided the clichéd architectural hotspots of Rome or Vienna, concentrating, instead, on the then neglected Spain and Mexico. Both countries engendered in him an interest in hybrid architecture; the Islamic/Iberian of Spain, the Aztec/Iberian of Mexico.

His response has been buildings sensible for the region. His inspiration, though, has not been the traditional Spanish-Pueblo style of the region or even Frank Lloyd Wright's Taliesin models. Predock has, instead, turned to the work of Luis Barragán, who found an architecture as authentic as Le Corbusier's but one that drew on regional or traditional influences. So, the colours and shapes of Predock's houses are intended to fit the desert. The concrete blocks of the Winandy residence, Scottsdale, Arizona (1990), for example, are made from an aggregate chosen to match the tone of the soil. Predock stresses that context turns buildings into 'abstract landscape'; indeed, he is registered as a landscape architect in New Mexico. This vision contrasts with that of another desert builder, Joshua Schweitzer, whose own architecture proposes no such thing (see The Monument, page 118).

Predock might not now touch adobe, but wants houses protected from the sun during the day and

Two towers rise from and above the front facade, signalling the meeting of the two axes (one north-south, the other east-west) which define the interior organization.

The exterior of the Winandy residence in Arizona blends with the surrounding landscape.

The covered entrance way (left). With such powerful sunlight, no architect could resist the opportunity to make patterns with the shadows. A similar philosophy inspired the pool at the core of the house (below) where the cool stillness of the space is broken only by the brittle entry of the sun.

the cold at night. He also considers the desert so overwhelming that homes should have only small windows from which to see it. Roofs are flat or barrel-vaulted. Where a tiled pitch has been forced by local laws, as with the Winandy residence, Predock avoided the neighbouring missionary-style red by personally choosing individual tiles from handmade batches. It adds up to a domestic architecture of thick building envelopes punctured by deeply recessed windows.

Such architecture would come across as admirable though rather dull, but for Predock's interest in ethnic forms. His fascination for these is expressed in the Fuller residence, Pinnacle Peak, Arizona (1985), where the powerful grandeur of the house is reduced by a silly, stepped pyramid containing one room. The Winandy residence embodies Predock's obsession with ancient Mexican mysticism less figuratively and more successfully. The setting sun can be viewed through a hole in a wall from the roof of the guest house, which is reached up a wide flight of steps. But Predock's inclusion of running water and geometric pools in the courtyards of his houses suggests his more effective exposure to Moorish architecture.

The Zuber residence condenses many of Predock's ideas into just one building. Perhaps the programme allowed for such clarity. The Zubers, with two grown-up sons, wanted an 'adult house';

The ethnic forms of the Fuller residence at Pinnacle Peak, Arizona

When lit at night by 1,000 underfloor lights, the simple deck is transformed into a runway from which to take off and explore the distant views of Phoenix.

The master bedroom is elevated above the rest of the house (left), one side overlooking the internal courtyard while the other has windows (below) that turn mere sleeping quarters into the bridge of the Starship Enterprise.

there was to be no family room or even a door to the master bedroom, and all public rooms were to be grand enough for the smartest of entertaining. Predock's task, therefore, was simplified to fitting a relatively small number of rooms on to a desert site high above Phoenix.

Perhaps he did. The house has two axes, perpendicular to each other. The shorter north–south one emerges out of the hillside with a cavernous study at ground level, the master bedroom above, a courtyard and then the dining room at the front of the house. The longer east–west axis is an enfilade of rooms from the garage, through the kitchen, to dining and living rooms. Two square towers in concrete blocks, set at an angle to the principal stucco façade, acknowledge the two axes.

The plan allows Predock to provide each room with a different outlook, even character. The study, for example, is set deep into the hillside. Its window overlooks water, which runs down, like a mountain spring, to the square- and diamond-shaped pools of the two cavernous courtyards which are reminiscent of Arabic architecture. The dining and living rooms, though, are thrust out into the landscape, their views of the desert framed by windows set deep in the walls and further protected from the sun by louvres.

The master bedroom, elevated above the rest of the house, is Predock's response to Judy Zuber's

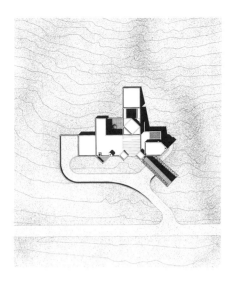

Site plan. Predock was so inspired by the location that he slept rough for several nights on the site before starting work. Such dedication allowed him to provide each room, on completion, with its own particular quality.

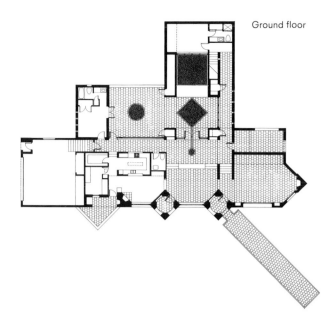

Ground floor

fantasy of a New York penthouse. The room is organized so that the Zubers can lie in bed, looking out to the mountains above Phoenix through windows straight out of a twenty-first-century spaceship: Predock, though immersed in the ethnic, has always had an interest in aeronautics after training for a year with McDonnell Aircraft.

That explains the bridge. The aubergine-coloured structure, intended as a gateway and viewing platform for the house, appears somewhat superfluous. But, at night, small gaps in the paving allow underfloor light to shine through, turning the bridge into a runway on the way to central Phoenix. As Sylvia Lavin has pointed out: 'the bridge that at first seemed to take you nowhere becomes a bridge ready to take you anywhere.'

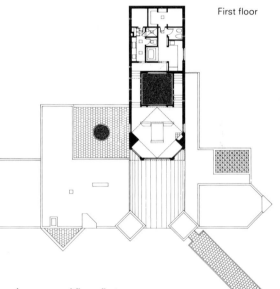

First floor

Floor plans: ground floor; first floor. In section (below) the house emerges out of its sloping location, providing both an intimate, shady zone of rooms and a brighter row of rooms which concentrate on the views.

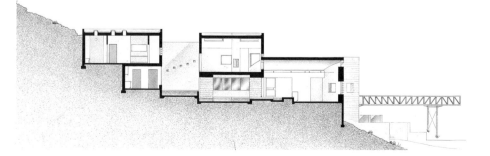

Alberto Campo Baeza
Casa Gaspar

Zahora, Cadiz, Spain, 1990–91

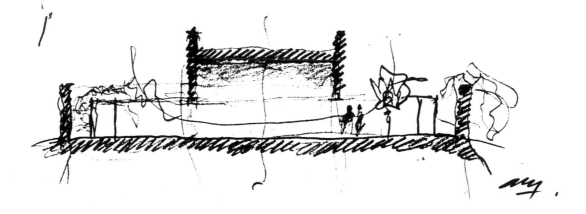

Unlike the work of his peers, Alberto Campo Baeza's architecture is not very Spanish. His houses, such as the Casa Gaspar, do not deal with the sort of issues common to a generation of Spanish architects who seek to fulfil the goals of a modernism that responds to local context and history. Such regionalist tendencies have characterized the post-Franco outburst of creativity perfectly represented by an architect such as Enric Miralles (see page 184). Campo Baeza, instead, works to more universal principles, re-editing the international style of pure white modernism.

His houses, clearly inspired by Le Corbusier's purist villas, are, therefore, somewhat old-fashioned. Indeed, Campo Baeza uses little new technology, and avoids spatial gymnastics and the sort of ideologies so popular with his generation. Nor does he explore the political or social agenda of modernism – the Gaspar house and his other houses are small, bourgeois residences. He stands out, though, because the ingenuity of his geometric volumes and logical floor plans reveal new subtleties for a traditional style of domestic architecture.

Campo Baeza proves that he is interested solely in the aesthetics of this type of modernism, using a language in which white equals light. 'In architecture, the colour white, even more clearly than in painting, is something more, much more, than a mere abstraction,' he says. 'It is a firm and

Although the majority of his Spanish peers have been inspired by regional tendencies, Campo Baeza has turned instead to the old-fashioned principles of classic, white modernism.

The relationship between the interior and the patios is crucial to the success of the house. Campo Baeza emphasizes the link through a series of devices such as the apparent continuation of materials, the inside and outside separated only by a frameless window.

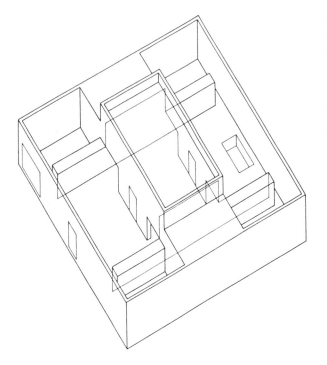

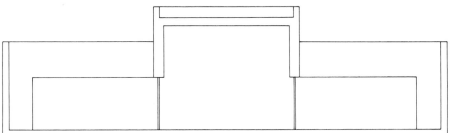

Campo Baeza sees controlling
and manipulating natural light
as part of the architect's role.
Windows for the interior are
arranged so that indirect,
rather than direct, light is
reflected off the surrounding
white walls – a device made
clear in the section (below).
The method also works
because of the generous
number of patios (left).

secure base, efficient in resolving problems of light, trapping it, reflecting it, making it fall upon things, making it slide.'

The process has its precedents. Henri Ciriani, France's leading Corb revivalist, sees white architecture as a historical inevitability. Architecture, set free from the necessity of walls through the all-glass façade inspired by Mies van der Rohe, must now concentrate on what quality of light should be shut out. Campo Baeza starts at this point, differentiating between horizontal and vertical, and direct and reflected light with ingenious sections.

The Casa Turagano (Madrid 1987), for example,

sits on a south-facing slope, and from the street looks like a three-storey house, but from the very private garden can be seen to have four storeys. The house is entered off the street, and the visitor walks straight into a mid-level comprising the kitchen and dining room, with the large sitting room below and bedrooms and rooftop pavilion above. Campo Baeza links these four floors with three double-height spaces, interlocking at the diagonal. Light filters to all parts of the house, either directly, through windows in the south façade, or indirectly, reflected off the white surfaces.

The Casa Gaspar plays much the same game but to different rules. The Casa Turagano sits on a hill

The earlier Casa Turagano
also allowed Campo Baeza to
manipulate light through the
organization of the section.
However, this house's urban
location made it necessarily
more sophisticated than the
Casa Gaspar.

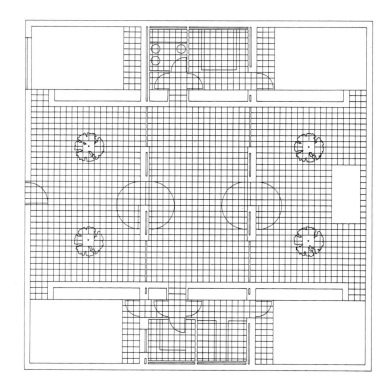

in the crowded city, the Gaspar on flat land in the middle of an orange grove. Campo Baeza's design for the Casa Gaspar had the scope to be far less dense than the city house, though the family wanted total privacy. So the Casa Gaspar is on only one level, its principal rooms – living/dining, two bedrooms, kitchen and bathroom – surrounded entirely by a 3 metre (9 feet, 10 inches) high wall, punctured only twice by a pedestrian entrance and garage door. The whole house is white and its brick walls are covered in painted render.

The rooms of the house lie in a strip through the middle of the compound, leaving on each side more than two-thirds of the site as patios. The

Floor plan (above): two patios, each with their own pair of orange trees, lie either side of the main living room. But even the bedrooms, both for the parents and children, have their own courtyards, each one made private by their massive walls.

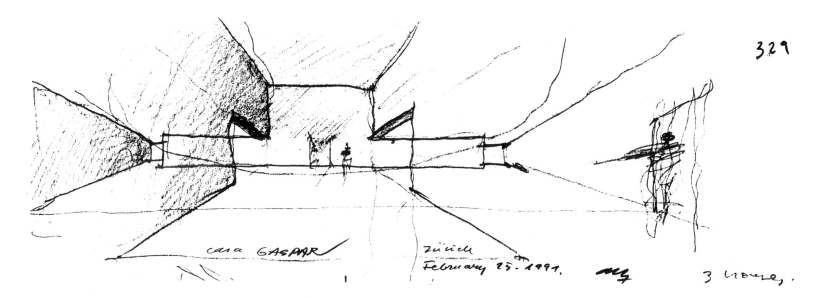

329

casa GASPAR   zürich
February 25. 1991.   3 houses.

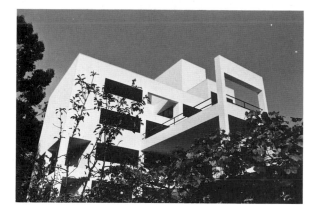

In his town hall at Fene-La Coruña, Campo Baeza was inspired by Giuseppe Terragni's Casa del Fascio at Como.

Campo Baeza achieves an admirable minimalist quality, one which is sought after by so many other contemporary architects. Indeed his personal slogan is 'more with less'.

living room has patios on either side, each one planted with two orange trees; but even the smaller rooms, such as bedrooms and kitchen, have their own spaces, separated from the main patio by a wall. The composition and proportions of the floor plan are far from casual.

One of Campo Baeza's numerous heroes is the Italian rationalist Giuseppe Terragni. His influence on Campo Baeza is most evident in an earlier work. The town hall of Fene-La Coruña (1980) has a composition of windows and white walls, drawing heavily on the proportional system of the façade of Terragni's Casa del Fascio in Como (1936). Campo Baeza cannot repeat this in elevation since the Casa Gaspar is a single-storey white box, but he can in plan. The length of the site is divided into three equal strips – 'proportion B B B/ open, closed, open'. The width of the site is also broken down into three parts, but 'proportion A 2A A/servant, served, servant'.

The Gaspar therefore differs from the Turagano in both section and plan; while the Madrid house had, through necessity, a vertical section and diagonal light, the Casa Gaspar has a horizontal section and horizontal light. Rooms are illuminated by light reflected off the high walls of the compound and not from above. Campo Baeza also achieves a clearer purity of form. The limestone floors, kept at exactly the same grade for the living room and patios, make each feature

appear to run into one another. The two large glass windows are inserted framelessly into the walls.

Both details produce an aesthetic of the absolute minimum, closer to the aspirations of John Pawson and Claudio Silvestrin's Neuendorf house (see page 28). Indeed, Campo Baeza has his own Zen-like mantra: 'Silence versus so much deafening noise. Simplicity versus so much complication. White and simple architecture attempts to achieve everything with almost nothing: more with less.'

Tadao Ando
Kidosaki house

Setagaya, Tokyo, Japan, 1982–86

The historical influences on Tadao Ando are clear.
The architect, at the age of 20, bought a
monograph of Le Corbusier's oeuvre and has
admitted to including many of the master's
principles in his work. The Kidosaki house in
Tokyo, for example, has a roof garden, continuous,
if not horizontal, windows, a free plan and a free
façade – four of Le Corbusier's 'five points' from
the 1920s.

But Ando's architecture is a product of far
deeper diversity. He belongs to a generation of
architects from the 1970s who began to question
the tenets of post-war modernism, rejecting its
tendency towards repetitiveness. Le Corbusier was
one influence but so were the historic buildings of
his home towns Osaka and Nara, where Japanese
architecture, traditionally horizontal non-
geometrical, created irregular spaces. 'In the end,
the simple box proposed by modernism is nothing
but a simple box. I want to enrich architecture by
introducing complexity into that simple box.'

To listen to Ando, you would think him
primarily an intellectual or an academic. But Ando

**A cool, calm modernist
approach, suitable for the
end of the twentieth century,
characterizes the Kidosaki
house where Ando has
exploited Le Corbusier's rules
to create a decent living
environment within the city.**

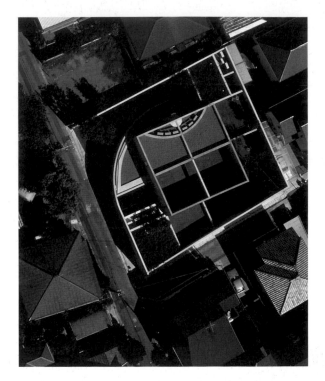

The Hyogo Children's Museum (top), which provides a platform from which to view the landscape, and the early Row house (above).

never qualified as an architect, coming to the profession through a career in boxing. Such a past goes some way towards explaining the somewhat sensual, physical approach of his architecture. 'It is important that I learn things through my own body and spirit rather than through books,' he says. For Ando also rejected the non-site-specific nature of post-war modernism, like Frank Lloyd Wright and Alvar Aalto before him. 'My architecture is based on the compositional methods and form of modernism,' says Ando. 'But I place importance on place.'

'To put it another way, I want to integrate dynamically two opposites, abstraction and representation. Abstraction is an aesthetic based on clarity of logic, and representation is concerned with all historical, cultural, climatic, topographic, urban and living conditions.' The result is an architecture almost entirely in perfectly shuttered concrete, its details in steel or wood.

In the country, his buildings are a stage. The Hyogo Children's Museum, for example, sets up a series of free-standing walls to frame views of the fantastic lakeside forests. In the city, his buildings are enclosures, cutting off the urban sprawl behind tall walls and creating oases of tree-filled courtyards. The Row house of 1975 – the building that first grabbed the world's attention – placed accommodation on either side of a central courtyard, forcing the inhabitants to go outside in

order to move from room to room and commune with wind, light, air and rain.

The Kidosaki house follows the pattern set up by Ando ten years earlier, but its size, and the character of its owners, produce an ultimately more sophisticated design. The clients were a married couple with two elderly relatives – Mr Kidosaki's father and Mrs Kidosaki's mother. The three households wanted to live together while maintaining their own privacy. Ando was the ideal architect. For yet another of his facets is the contrast between the purity of his geometric walls set against the messier actions of everyday living. 'The building remains a simple box, but nature and human movement alter the architecture in complex ways.'

The main part of the house fills a three-storey cube set at the centre of the site, characteristically surrounded by a tall wall along the property line. The wall curves away from the street in front, indicating the entrance to the house. At this point, a wide flight of steps leads down to a shady entrance courtyard from which the parents' quarters are entered through two doors. Another, narrower flight of stairs leads upwards to the couple/children's rooms.

Inside, the three variously sized apartments are a collection of tightly overlapping rooms which lock together like a Rubik cube. One lower-level apartment, to the east, has a two-storey sitting

Ando's carefully planned organization means that each principal room has a view of a calm and private courtyard.

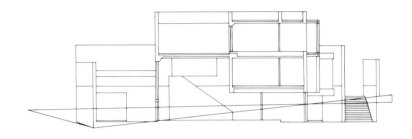

room, its extra height providing a spatial connection between parent and child. The apartment next door, to the west, does not have such apparent luxury but its bedroom is upstairs, parallel to the couple/children's quarters – another family link, though of a different kind.

The couple/children's apartment takes up most of the second level. There is the living room and dining area. But another flight of stairs leads up to the third level. Here, half the floor space is given over to bedrooms, while the other half is a courtyard. Indeed, the success of the house relies on its courtyards. The gap between the perimeter wall and the core creates a variety of spaces: the entrance garden to the north; a large courtyard to the south. The two elements provide both downstairs apartments with views. The upper apartment also has its own courtyards – the one on the roof, but also two others at either end of the living room.

These are all intensely private spaces, cut off from the streets outside and from relatives by walls. Each one is planted with trees, vines or shrubs. Ando cannot frame views of fantastic country scenes but he can concentrate the inhabitants' attention on to the beauty possible from one perfectly formed tree, the only possible sign of nature within a city. And just as the Row house places a courtyard inconveniently in the middle of the house, the complicated matrix of the

Kidosaki house allows for contained outdoor spaces in the most unexpected of places.

The result is an optical illusion like the library in Umberto Eco's *The Name of the Rose*. There, the plain, though massive walls of the building enclose a maze of staircases and bookshelves, each one connected to another through a complex arrangement of routes. The walls, however, also have a more metaphysical role, keeping potentially explosive ideas away from public exposure. In the same way, Ando maintains the privacy of the family. 'I wanted to create living spaces,' says Ando, 'simple shells on the outside and labyrinthine inside.'

Looking into one of the two apartments.

Basement

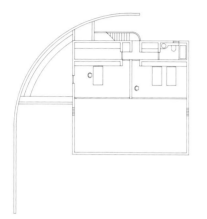

First floor

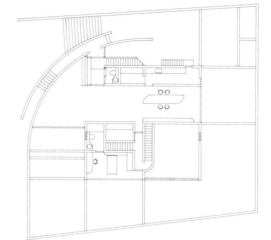

Ground floor

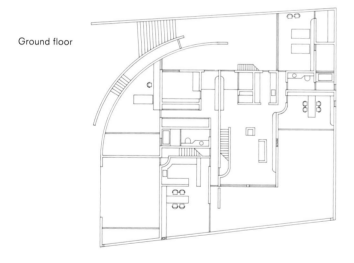

Roof

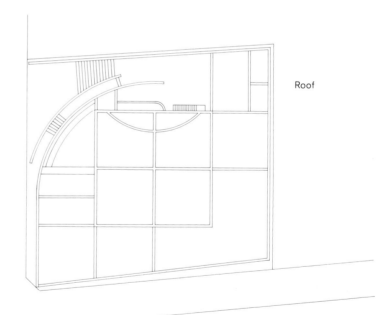

**Floor plans: basement;
ground floor, living room
and dining area; first floor,
bedrooms and courtyard;
roof, courtyards; .**

Chapter 2

Structural solutions

Mies van der Rohe, Farnsworth house, Plano, Fox River, Illinois, 1950 (left). Mies van der Rohe, Riehl house, Neubabelsberg, Potsdam, 1907 (below).

Just like the model villa (see pages 20–27), so modern architecture as the exploration of structure has followed two parallel paths of historical development. One follows the unbending rules of composition, scale and location to achieve the classical purity possible through structure; the pavilions of Ludwig Mies van der Rohe (1886–1969), for example, bear comparison with the rigidity of Le Corbusier. The other takes a less dogmatic approach, achieving an equivalent honesty, if not grandeur, through pragmatism; resulting most notably in the Case Study Houses of the post-war era, which respond to location and the individuality of the client as skilfully as the later work of Luis Barragán.

And just as the links between Le Corbusier and Palladio explain the essence of the model villa, so Mies' particular influence on architecture as the exploration of structure can be explained by his own more direct connections to an earlier architect's buildings and ideas. Mies trained with Peter Behrens (1868–1940) for three years from 1908. His master exposed him to the great Prussian architect Karl Friedrich Schinkel (1781–1841), whose own work, such as the Pavilion at the Charlottenhof Palace in Potsdam (1826), proffered an idealization of open space and the importance of the podium.

The impact of Schinkel on the young Mies can be seen in his early Riehl house in Potsdam (1907),

where a vernacular gable reads as a pediment above a scarcely disguised portico of columns. The whole house is then raised above the surrounding garden behind a retaining wall; in other words, a temple standing on its podium. Half a century later, Mies' New National Gallery in Berlin (1962–68) expressed similar sentiments in a vastly altered language of steel and glass.

Mies' two great houses, the Tugendhat villa in Brno, the Czech Republic (1930), and the Farnsworth House, Illinois (1950), clarified Mies' minimalist ideas. The earlier house, one storey to the street behind, two storeys to the garden in front, was raised on a podium. The garden façade comprised a continuous run of windows, of which every alternate one could be lowered into the ground. The result was an interior almost instantly made part of the exterior. The Farnsworth House, meanwhile, returned to the honesty of Hendrik Berlage (1856–1934), another of Mies' teachers, with eight steel columns welded to the fascias of the floor and roof planes, 'bypassing and touching but not resting on them so that the house appears to be slung between the vertical supports'.

The result was 'the proposition that a house can be a single architectural idea',[2] where the open space desired by Schinkel was made real; proof that mere structure could recreate the formality of Classicism. That ideal has informed architects ever since. Philip Johnson's Glass House (1949) took the

Stéphane Beel, Villa Maesen,
Zedelgem, 1989-92.

logic of Farnsworth to the extreme, providing the
iconic example of the one room building.
A younger generation has returned to Mies, seeking
a similar clarity.

Stéphane Beel's Villa Maesen near Bruges
(see page 79) comes close to Mies' ideas with a
consistent ground plan and predominance of
glazing to one side of the house. Beel apes Mies'
form as a means to produce a family home.
Children, at one end of the house, are constantly in
view though distant enough to be unheard. It is,
however, ironic that Mies' influence on other
architects has remained more consistent for public
than domestic work, though his reputation so
strongly rests on his houses.

The reason lies, perhaps, with the nature of the
late twentieth-century client. The Miesian pavilion,
with its glass-filled, steel frame, provides plenty of
natural light and scarcely any barrier between the
interior and exterior, but little privacy. That is fine
in the country or the suburb. Beel's Villa Maesen
looks on to a lawn surrounded by tall
rhododendrons. Nonda Katsalidis' beach house (see
page 175) enjoys some fantastic views of the sea,
though is sufficiently far from any other
habitation to make it work.

This dilemma – the near impossibility of
combining minimalist interiors, open to the
exterior, with privacy – is made clear by its solution
in a house outside Antwerp, by Xaveer de Geyter.

Mies van der Rohe, Tugendhat House, Brno, 1930 (left). Philip Johnson, Glass House, New Canaan, Connecticut, 1949 (below).

This boasts a steel portal which converts some of the main rooms into full- time conservatories. Yet, de Geyter is forced to make this the garden façade, obscuring the rest of the house from the street behind a sand dune (see page 162).The dilemma can scarcely be solved in the city. Only a Japanese architect such as Shinichi Ogawa (see page 94) seems prepared to stick rigidly to dogma, forcing his client to live in an all-glass cube.

The Case Study Houses offer an alternative source of inspiration to architects; a realm of pragmatism where the diversity of contemporary life can be reflected. The process started with the purchase of an obscure Californian magazine in 1937 by John Entenza. The new owner also became editor, renaming the magazine *Arts & Architecture*. As the war ended, Entenza organized and commissioned a series of experimental houses by some of California's leading architects such as Richard Neutra, Raphael Soriano, Charles Eames and Craig Ellwood. The first few completed houses paid homage to the 1930s, 'when building stalled and theory flourished'.[3]

Each house was a marvellous statement of Californian lifestyles: open-plan interiors, car ports and often generous and well-landscaped gardens. The floor plans, with their parallel arrangement of rooms, hinted at Frank Lloyd Wright's Prairie houses or the horizontal and vertical planes of the interior of Mies' German pavilion for the Barcelona Expo (1929). More important, however, was the pursuit of architecture through standardization and prototype. The Case Study Houses were to be a means of producing good mass housing, in response to a post-war shortage. The war had also caused all sorts of problems in the supply of building materials. Entenza's goal was a prototype architecture where each house was constructed from simple, mass-produced factory products that were readily available.

Charles and Ray Eames' own house in Pacific Palisades (1949), for example, was to have been a bridge structure but was changed on site to two volumes either side of a central courtyard, where prefabricated parts build up into a two-storey steel cage opening on to a meadow in front. Forty years later, Daryl Jackson achieved much the same thing (see page 89). His beach house was constructed gradually around four sides of an existing 1950s bungalow. The resulting form is a courtyard house which, just like those houses in California, reflects the relaxed lifestyle of the Jackson family far more closely than a predominantly brick-built structure. The house was also constructed with those industrial or natural products available, not because of some post-war shortage but owing to the difficulty of transporting materials to a remote Australian location.

The prototypical ambition of the Case Study Houses has also become absorbed into the

Mies van der Rohe,
Barcelonata pavilion,
Barcelona, 1929.

European avant-garde. Eames' success at Pacific Palisades rests largely with his ability to break away from the purity of Miesian materials or the rigidity of the Miesian pavilion. The legitimization of materials used not simply for purely constructional purposes informs the houses by OMA (see page 103) or Dirk Alten (see page 93), both architects using wooden panels or corrugated steel sheets to clad their buildings. And the Wrightian/Miesian arrangement of parallel rooms is used not only in plan but also in section, creating interiors where overlapping spaces reflect a less formal contemporary lifestyle.

Thus the Case Study Houses offered a model for modern living. Mies' European houses, like those of Le Corbusier or Frank Lloyd Wright, were still homes for a rapidly disappearing, hierarchical society, where servants, if not housed on site, were provided with generous quarters for domestic preparation. The Case Study Houses, for the first time, made architects concentrate on the small, single family houses of the average American household.

But there is also a central irony. Entenza's solution to a post-war housing shortage through good, cheap solutions, created, instead, a new style of architectural one-offs where the rich of California could display their new found wealth through the new architecture. Today's examples of private houses inspired by the Case Study Houses suffer no such contradiction. This pragmatic approach to

structure has no relation whatsoever to any social goal. Instead, architects look to Eames, just as others turn to Barragán, to find a stylistic solution to the variety of lifestyles of contemporary clients and as a greater sign of respect to location. Aesthetics, not altruism, informs their judgements.

1. Johnson, Philip. *Mies van der Rohe*. London: Secker & Warburg, 1978.
2. Dunster, David. *Key buildings of the 20th century. 2, Houses 1945–89*. London: Butterworth Architecture, 1990.
3. McCoy, Esther. *Case study houses 1945–62*. Los Angeles, CA: Hennessey & Ingalls, 1977.

Stéphane Beel's Villa
Maesen (right and far right)
fulfils a firmly rational
objective and yet fits quite
comfortably within an old
garden, surrounded by trees.

Stéphane Beel
Villa Maesen

Zedelgem, Belgium, 1989–92

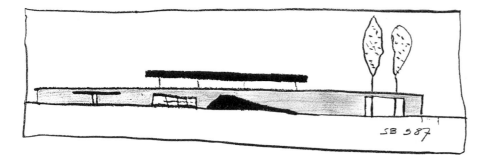

Stéphane Beel's houses are usually located within the modernist tradition of the Low Countries. The Villa Maesen is something of an exception. Its single volume suggests the concept of the house as pavilion like Mies van der Rohe's Farnsworth house (1946–50); an association that is strengthened by the rectilinear plan and flat slab of Beel's house. Its cedar cladding and articulated window voids, however, place it closer in appearance to Marcel Breuer's own house in New Canaan (1947).

These references, to American structural types rather than European abstraction, mark out the Villa Maesen as different. The Flemish-speaking areas of the Low Countries have suffered scarcely any break in the development of a rationalist, modern architecture between the heroic period of the inter-war years and today, except for the architecture of OMA (see page 100). Architects have habitually returned to their national architectural heroes such as Willem Dudok or Gerrit Rietveld for inspiration, developing and enriching the international style for both public and private work. Beel's work normally conforms to this national stereotype.

A villa in Brasschaat (1992), next door to that by Xaveer de Geyter (see page 166), was designed and built almost contemporaneously with the Villa Maesen. Yet, the two villas are fundamentally different. The Brasschaat villa is a more traditional two-storey house sitting centrally on its plot; Beel

Cutaways achieve a variety of ends. Some are windows, others have more sophisticated purposes such as forming this pleasant, outdoor, breakfast area.

The BAC bank in Bruges
(left) and the villa at
Brasschaat (above).

displays his characteristic use of white render, and
small outdoor patios are placed around the
perimeter of the house where views of the garden
are framed by vertical white planes. This feature,
characteristic even of Beel's public work such as
the BAC bank in Bruges, creates small, intensely
private courtyards not dissimilar to those found in
Tadao Ando's work (see page 70).

Beel's scheme for the Villa Maesen indicates a
radical shift in his domestic architecture, taking a
fundamentally different approach to planning and
construction. His leap of style can be explained on
aesthetic rather than intellectual grounds; a two-
storey, white rendered villa would have stood out
far too much, for the house stands in the grounds
of an old castle surrounded by its plantations of fir
and rhododendrons. The Maesen family bought a
plot on the estate in the old kitchen gardens

**Rear elevation. Beel formed
a space between the house
and its adjacent wall which
recreates exactly the volume
of the real house. The
resulting enclosed corridor
is in direct contrast to the
more open garden side.**

The house runs parallel to one garden wall and continues beyond another, which approaches at a right angle. Thus the inhabitants have views not simply of one garden, but of two.

reached up the original beech-lined drive of the castle. Tall brick walls still stand, one running along the back of the site, and another, perpendicular to the first, dividing the plot into two.

Beel saw that a new building would have to be sufficiently minimal to leave the site largely unchallenged. His response was to create one rectangular volume, 7 metres (22 feet, 11 inches) wide and 60 metres (196 feet, 10 inches) long, while the cedar panelling, neutral volume, and flat slab of this house provide the kitchen garden with what Beel calls 'just another wall, but inhabited'. The construction uses steel and cladding rather than the rendered concrete slabs of his pure white villas. The building is raised on a concrete slab, partly over a basement garage and store rooms. Steel I-beams carry the roof. The main walls are clad in vertical cedar boards while the return walls of the small patios are clad in aluminium panels.

The neatness of the cladding – where wall and roof meet so smoothly that no overhang exists – recalls one of the qualities of some of the later Case Study Houses. The deep windows and patios, set back from the flat plane of the garden façade, gouge incisions in what is otherwise a solid cylinder. The almost structural device recalls Breuer's own house, an association further emphasized by Beel's similar use of cedar panelling.

The house is placed towards the back of the site, parallel to the rear wall but exactly 7 metres (22

feet, 11 inches) from it so that the gap recreates the volume of the house exactly. The last few metres of the house are too long to fit into just one of the two kitchen gardens, so a gap has been created in the dividing wall, through which the house extends, allowing views of both kitchen gardens. The proximity of the walls logically indicated where Beel placed the front and the back of the house and therefore the internal layout.

The empty volume along the back of the house does not produce great views. The rear elevation reflects this with very few windows but the space does provide a suitably protected sense of arrival. The front door is approached along a row of broken flag stones laid at the bottom of the wall, then up an *in situ* concrete ramp to an entrance podium. The location of the house leaves the rest of the garden largely untouched. The front elevation responds with one huge oblong panel cut out and replaced by a terrace and sliding doors, and another section of the façade replaced by the low window of the children's play area.

The layout inside also reflects the proximity of the wall behind. The children's bedrooms, bathrooms and kitchen run along the back of the house, leaving the front as one open-plan sweep of rooms overlooking the gardens. But the floor plan also demolishes any clichéd concept of rooms, replacing them with an informal enfilade of areas possible for any use. 'The inside volumes', says Beel,

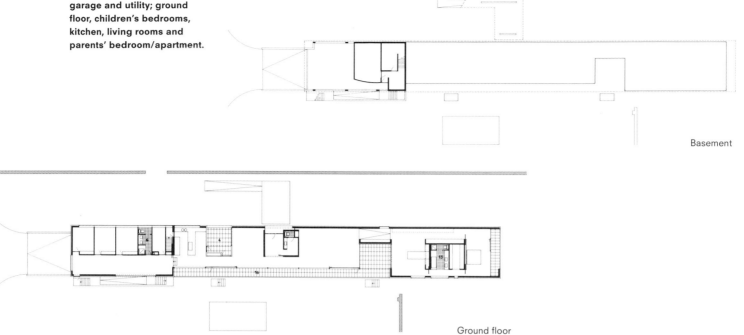

Basement

Ground floor

'are like big pieces of furniture that grade privacy and assembly, open and used, inside and out.'

The views are everything. The difference between the halves of the divided plot is maximized – one half planted as a formal garden, the other as an orchard. People walking through the house are, therefore, travelling through a constantly changing landscape. Equally important are the views between the separate parts of the house. The open plan of the house allows parents to keep an eye on their children, despite the two parts of the family being at either end of the house.

Small patios, not too dissimilar from those around the villa in Brasschaat, continue the visual axis through the house; people in the dining area can see activities in the kitchen across the breakfast patio. More significantly, the insertion of the patios and outside terraces between the functions enforces further the differences between areas, ranged one after another along the house. 'The patios', says Beel, 'are outdoor rooms that mediate distance and closeness.'

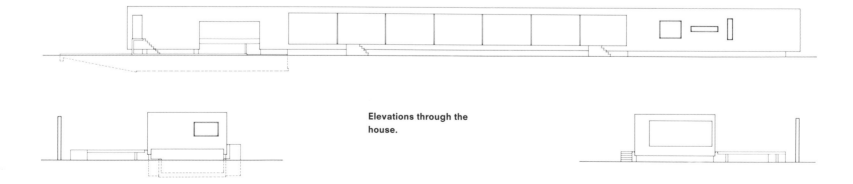

Elevations through the house.

Daryl Jackson
Beach house

Bermagui, NSW, Australia, 1989–90

The beach house (opposite) sits comfortably on the top of a small hill beside a tidal lake (below). Yet respect for context has not stopped Daryl Jackson from exploring an architecture reliant on structure.

Both Daryl Jackson and Barrie Marshall have designed beach houses around courtyards, though the differences between the two are far more evident than their similarities. Marshall's house (see page 120) is generated primarily by its context. Jackson's house, though placed with exquisite taste, emphasizes architecture as a system of construction.

Jackson runs an international practice of architects whose commissions since the mid-1960s, often large commercial buildings, reveal a wide variety of styles. Yet, he has tried to design one private house a year: 'since the process of feedback is more readily apparent than from public commissions, though I'll only do one if a client wants to experiment', he says. Ironically, the freedom represented by his domestic commissions has not encouraged further diversity. The work has, instead, inspired Jackson with a series of themes from which he has distilled a consistent architectural form.

The catalogue starts with the Abrahams house in Brighton, Melbourne (1977). The more traditional pitched roofs of its neighbours are translated into a series of perpendicular elements clipped to the house, like a lean-to. The gap created between the more solid core and the skeletal framework shades the ground-floor patios and, with tiles removed, provides deep coves to upstairs windows. A roof-light, running parallel to a

staircase below, splits the upper floors into two – one side for the parents, the other for the children.

These ideas are taken further with Jackson's own weekend house in Shoreham outside Melbourne (1978). Two shed-like structures, one a three-storey house, the other a stable-block, appear to have been carved out of the same element and then separated. A terrace, partly raised on wooden beams, connects the two. Here, the lean-tos of the Abrahams house, 'usually a comfortable add-on affair, are lifted from the humble back porch or filled-in veranda to become the whole dwelling', says Jackson. Baton upon baton of green timber support the sheets of corrugated iron for the roofs, whose incline mirrors the land fall.

The beach house is a development of certain ideas originally formed by Jackson in earlier projects, such as the Abrahams house (top) and the Cox house (above).

The Cox house in Hawthorn (1980) takes the next logical step. Jackson still finds space on the suburban plot to place a long swimming pool beside the house by cutting away parts of the building's perimeter footprint. A strongly linear length of lattice sunshades supported on metal poles marks the halfway point on the site. More significantly, the device shows the development of Jackson's lean-tos into a vertical position, where their role in protecting against the heat of the sun is far less important than their abstract qualities.

The house at Bermagui makes references to this earlier work but strengthens each element into a recognizable architectural form. Jackson has designed his house so that it consciously contradicts the internalized living of the city. The area, on the coast but seven hours' drive from either Melbourne or Sydney, has a reasonable 22–25° climate all year round, ensuring an almost constant outdoor life; living in the house thus becomes something approximating to camping. Jackson emphasizes this lifestyle in the design by a collection of rooms gathered around a courtyard. The house is located on the top of a small hill, sitting beside a tidal lake behind a dune.

An old 1950s bungalow (demolished once the new house was habitable) sat at the centre of the site, and the new building has developed around the old. A 3.5 metre (11 feet, 5 inches) high concrete block wall surrounds the courtyard on almost four

sides, cement rendered in a colour that ensures that no one could take it to be made from natural rock. A vertebrate roof structure, with exposed beams and tie rods, made from green hardwood and clad in corrugated iron, creates a consistent section. The pitched roof repeats the contour of the surrounding land.

Rooms are then elaborated like lean-tos, clipped on to the masonry wall where necessary; a living room overlooking the lake, a study on one side, a master bedroom on another. Four guest bedrooms are laid out in a line, with a garage at one end, set at an angle to the main courtyard. Two bathrooms, for the guest rooms, are stand-alone blocks, acting as gatehouses through which the courtyard is entered. There is something deliberately provisional about the whole house. Rooms are not connected by neat indoor corridors; instead people are forced out of doors, passing under the open, though sheltered, colonnades. The guest bedrooms are big, empty spaces, leaving people to bed down as they will.

Each room has a series of glass and flywired panels in frames, moved like screens, to protect against the wind and bugs. Panels of corrugated iron, mounted horizontally and slightly forward from the building's walls, act as sunshades. Two huge water tanks, mounted on two corners of the courtyards, are far from symbolic. Each day often ends in an evening thunderstorm, cutting off the electricity supply and therefore the water. The

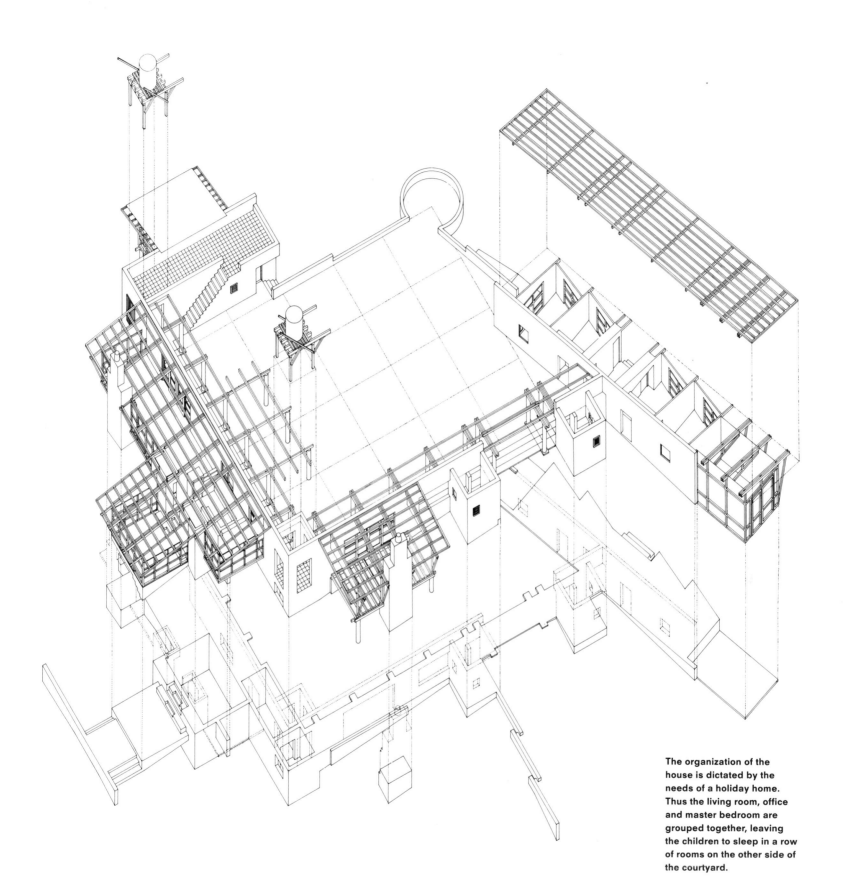

The organization of the
house is dictated by the
needs of a holiday home.
Thus the living room, office
and master bedroom are
grouped together, leaving
the children to sleep in a row
of rooms on the other side of
the courtyard.

Even the interior picks up on elements of Jackson's other houses. The ceiling of exposed timbers recalls Jackson's weekend house, while the vertical panels used as sunshades are a reminder of the Cox house. However, the beach house, accommodating the rhythm and manners of a vacation home, generally enjoys a more relaxed appearance.

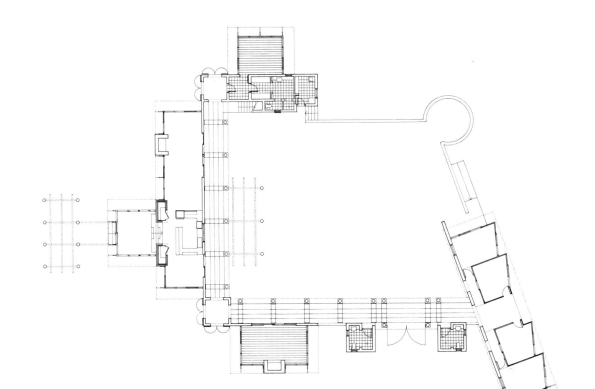

tanks, filled from an underground reservoir, supply the house with gravity-fed water when necessary.

Precedents for Bermagui can be seen in Jackson's earlier houses: the separation of parents from children in the Abrahams house: the inclined roof and untreated timber in Jackson's weekend house; and the vertical panels as sunshades in the Cox house. There are also parallels with the Californian Case Study Houses, a link strengthened by the simplicity of a holiday home, the distance from centres of production and, therefore, the necessity for something of a pre-assembled building. The structure of Jackson's house, assembled from mass-produced products and materials, resembles the Case Study Houses, which were originally intended to be constructed simply and *en masse* from a kit of parts, easily produced by converting Los Angeles wartime factories to peacetime production. Bermagui might not be constructed from factory products common to Los Angeles, but the water tanks, green timber, corrugated iron and flywire frames are the Australian outback equivalent.

The final form of Bermagui also enjoys a certain pragmatism, like another canonical Case Study House: the oft-repeated story of Eames converting his Case Study House on site from a bridge structure into two volumes either side of a court rings true for Jackson's house replacing the old bungalow, the roofscape rising and falling with the land and the two bathrooms as gatehouses.

And finally, there is an elevation of the normally banal object to art. Richard Neutra mounted an old Ford Model A spotlight in the sitting room of his Lovell Health house (1929) – a demonstration house pre-dating the Case Study Houses by 15 years. Similarly, Jackson, seeking a means of letting light into the interior of rooms, turns not to some fashionable glazed brick, but to simple terracotta drainpipes, their ends sawn off and mounted at eye-level in the bedrooms. The pipes do the job but also introduce an almost decorative motif into the grey, rendered walls.

Rooms are arranged around a central courtyard. Each one is entered, not through adjoining doors, but beneath sheltered colonnades.

Dirk Alten
The Eagle

Braunschweig, Germany, 1989–92

Theoretically the Eagle is little more than a two-storey extension to a suburban villa. Yet Dirk Alten, its architect, sees his task as to differentiate the new from the old. As a result his house looks like something dropped from the sky, contrasting with its neighbours not only in its flat roof (opposite) but also in its pursuit of abstract games rather than suburban sensibilities. The shutters, for example, merely through their everyday action of opening and closing, have a serious sculptural aspect.

Where can you fit in a new house, asks Dirk Alten, when all available space has been filled? And what is appropriate for a German town such as Braunschweig, where a century's prosperity has filled the suburbs with a profusion of pitched roofs and detached villas? The answer would suggest that the Eagle is a house compromised by its urban surroundings.

The new house is placed on top of the garage of an existing adjacent villa, where it will look as if it 'has fallen from the sky or has been carefully set down by a crane'. Alten's uncompromising stand sets up a deliberate contrast between both buildings. 'The supposed absurdity of this landing springs a dance between two postures,' says Alten, referring to the conventional home set against the alien form of a cube. The difference between the two lies not just in shapes.

Alten's architectural theme sees 'a building as a spatial story, capable of developing its own means of communication'. He cites, as an example of 'stories of space', English landscape gardens, where the clearings cut from the woods create rooms in the open. The Eagle, therefore, contrasts even more with its neighbours. The existing houses follow convention in appearance and shape, but the Eagle is formed by having its pure geometry violated by the activities of its inhabitants. 'The traces left behind are the signs forming the appearance of the house,' says Alten. 'Solidified in formalism,' he

The extension sits on an existing garage and is entered under a cantilever and up a flight of stairs at the back of the house (left). The entrance is 'like an open wound' gouged from the main body of the house (below) while, inside, the kitchen unit is the only division within the open plan living room.

adds, 'the pitched roofs of the neighbours can only quote the activities which the intruder, the Eagle, landed in their midst, happily provides for its owner.'

The Eagle, therefore, ignores its context to such an extent that it cannot be seen as a house dictated by its surroundings. The building comes from an entirely different direction instead. Alten used to work for the Office of Metropolitan Architecture. He, like Xaveer de Geyter (see page 162), was there exposed to two impulses: the ability of the city to push a project to an extreme and, more importantly, the great break of European modernism from solid masonry to lightweight structure.

Alten's architectural agenda of volume defined by function is made possible by the building's structure. A balloon frame carries the main mass of the house, allowing for a relatively lightweight construction. One part of the cube is cantilevered over the perimeter of the garage below. The overhang creates a partially covered space, indicated by a thin, horizontal strip of blue, which is the Eagle's 'entrance hall', though it is outdoors.

A staircase, with metal mesh treads, rises beyond the footprint of the house to the upper storey. Here, a landing, set at 180° to the stairs, turns back to the front door, cutting through the skin of the box and revealing the layering of the structure 'like an open wound'. The solid walls of the bathroom lie on one side, the open windows of the kitchen on the other. Inside, rooms are partitioned by sliding doors or

Floor plans and elevations. Ground floor First floor

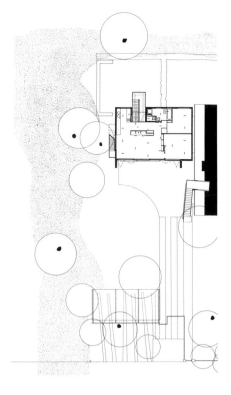

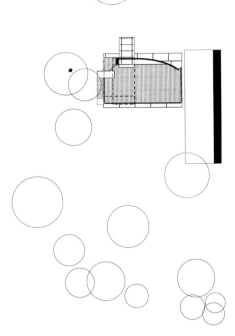

shelf units, leaving the floor space as intact as possible, an impression emphasized by an unbroken grid of neon strip lights fixed to the ceiling. A door from the living room gives access to another flight of stairs up to the roof terrace, where a double wall, both curved and sloping, tidies away outdoor clutter and supports the corrugated canopy to the front door downstairs.

The most dramatic violation of Alten's cube is, however, kept for the street façade. The structure is clad in equally lightweight natural plywood panels. Their manufactured smoothness and machine-made planes emphasize the abstraction of the cube, endangered only by the likelihood of windows. Alten, therefore, places the windows in a long, low strip, dividing the front of the house into three. These windows, despite such manipulated form, can still be swept from view by a series of plywood shutters which concertina open or closed across the façade, restoring the cube to its former purity.

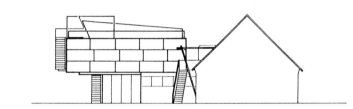

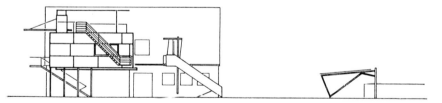

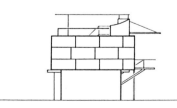

Shinichi Ogawa
Cubist house

Yamaguchi, Japan, 1990

The Cubist house is exactly that – an uncompromisingly rational frame infilled with glass (opposite), which has little, if any, regard for its inhabitant's needs of privacy and shade, despite its position within a typical Japanese city block (above).

The sheer severity of the Cubist house would suggest that Shinichi Ogawa's work is on the cutting edge of the Japanese avant-garde. Indeed, the majority of his generation have been given something of a historic opportunity in which to develop and experiment.

Ogawa belongs to the 'Next Wave', a group of architects, including Hajime Yatsuka (see page 228), waiting to take the positions held by the 'Middle Generation' of Tadao Ando (see page 65) or Toyo Ito. They, in turn, will shortly inherit the mantle of the 'Masters' such as Arata Isozaki, Fumihiko Maki, Kisho Kurokawa and the octogenarian Kenzo Tange. The younger generation of architects, patiently biding their time for large public commissions, are offered a number of opportunities to design private houses by the country's recently booming economy.

The Cubist house, therefore, fulfils most of these criteria. The client is a successful computer programmer specializing in 3-D and industrial design. The site is a typical Japanese house plot, squeezed into the generally low-grade muddle which makes up much of the urban fabric. And Ogawa's obsessions rest with an intellectual justification and an aesthetic manipulation of technology's constant race.

'Architecture gives form to technology from the human standpoint,' he says, adding that 'its solutions are highly ordered assemblages of a large number of complementary systems.' He revels in a list of more than 30 'data words', such as 'magnetism, geometry, mathematics' or 'SFX, robots, computers, LSI', the potential for gobbledegook reduced by the credibility of the 'programme' created for the lifestyle of the inhabitant.

A 6 metre (19 feet, 8 inches) cube occupies the site. It is entirely covered in glass, the panels fixed to a 1 metre (3 feet, 3 inches) grid of mullions. The interior space is then partitioned by four smaller cubes – something Ogawa calls 'big furniture'. Two of the cubes contain an enclosed room, referred to as studio B, the third, the bathroom and the fourth, the kitchen. A ramp, turning five times around the central block before it reaches the upper level, has a sloping floor made of transparent, perforated, stainless-steel panels, its five landings in glass.

The building's main working/living area, studio A, sits on top of the four smaller cubes, its smooth white floor divided by the glazed seams of the partitions below. Ogawa had intended to add an industrial turntable fitted with computers so that the client could more easily carry out a variety of projects simultaneously, but the budget had run out.

Interpreting Ogawa's architecture as merely part of Japan's new avant-garde is, however, to ignore its precedents. The key to the roots of this house lies in the work of Adolfo Natalini's Superstudio, a 1960s group of Italian rationalists. Their 'Catalog of villas' (1968–70) included designs for a vast variety of

Although expected to use this elevated level, its exposed position probably means that the inhabitant of the Cubist house spends more time in the private, though unpleasantly crowded, downstairs rooms.

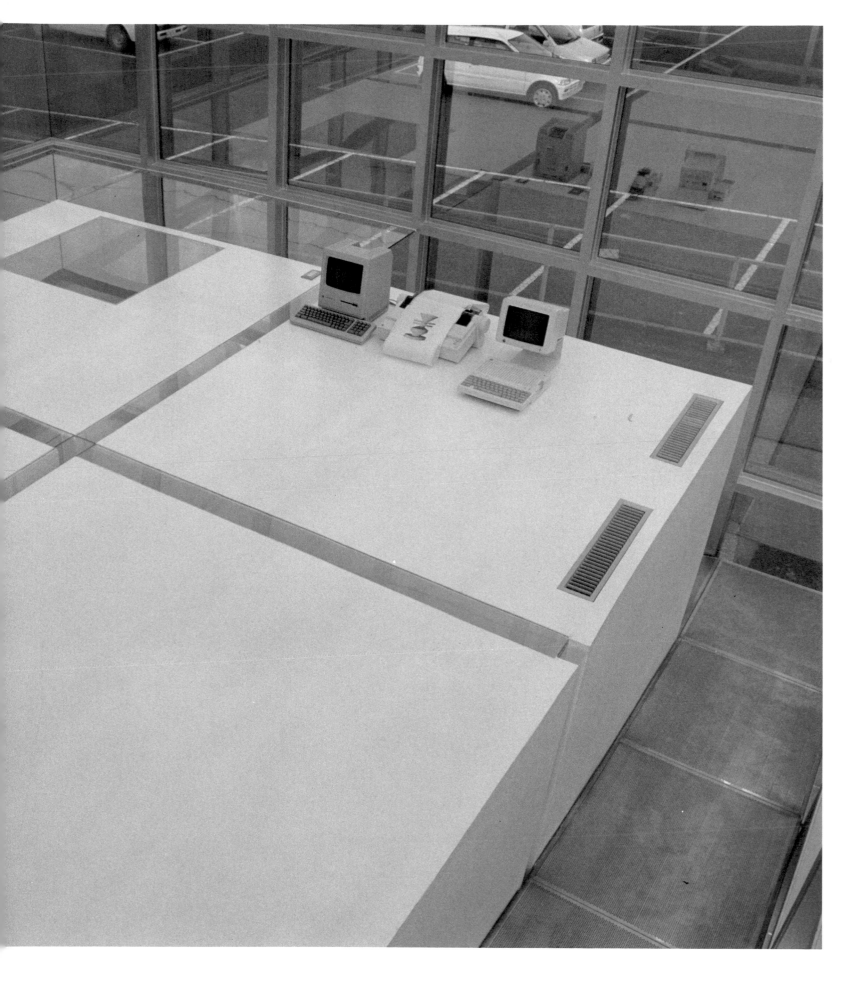

Section (right) and elevation (far right) of the Cubist house. The dimensions of the rooms inside and the furniture follow that of the frame absolutely.

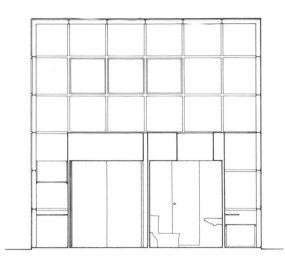

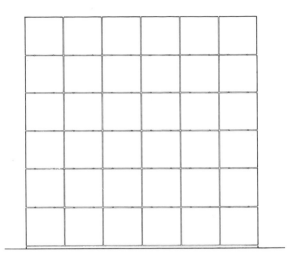

different housing types. Each one was presented as an axonometric, its surface covered in a dense rationalist grid for measurability.

Natalini's vision had limited appeal. The Italian architect created a whole series of images where the world was covered or organized by fantastic grids, such as 'Il monumento continuo' or 'The twelve ideal cities'. A series of furniture – Misura, by Zanotta – was enormously popular, its designer taking delight in making the corner of a table, for example, coincide exactly with the division of the grid.

Most importantly, Arata Isozaki visited Superstudio in 1971. The following year, the Japanese architect produced drawings for the Fukuoka Mutual Bank (1972–73), where the final design was developed from one gridded block, through a series of six sketches, into the final design. These ideas were taken up by lesser Japanese architects such as Fujii Hirome, whose houses Suzuki Tei and Miyajima Tei undergo a similar design development.

The Cubist house, in this light, is not so much part of Japan's burgeoning avant-garde but a revivalist style. The footprint of the house coincides exactly with the 6 metre (19 feet, 8 inches) structural grid, just like the furniture of Superstudio. Heinrich Klotz, the post-modern apologist, argues that Isozaki's exposure to Superstudio: 'helped Isozaki to break away from

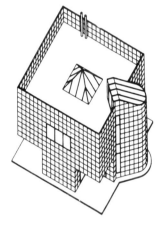

The work of the Florence-based architectural group Superstudio (left) has had a significant impact on the buildings of Isozaki (below) and Ogawa (right).

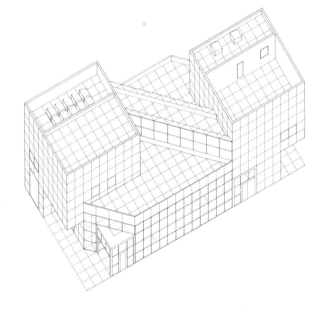

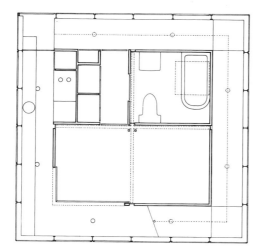

Ground floor

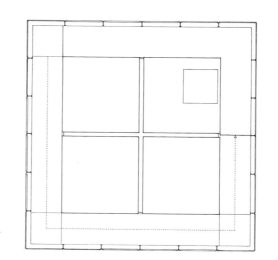

First floor

Floor plans: ground floor (far left), toilet, kitchen and bedroom; first floor (left) with its impossibly exposed working environment.

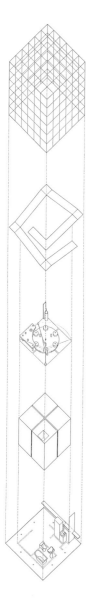

the brutalist tradition of Kenzo Tange and to advance [sic] into post-modernism'.

Ogawa's interest in technology has led to a very different position – a rationalist, and therefore appropriate, interpretation of Miesian constructional aesthetics. The Cubist house can be read as a one-room house, like Mies' Farnsworth house, where the furniture, those smaller cubes, is the only partitioning device, as in Johnson's Glass House. What also distances Ogawa from his peers and places him closer to his past, is his uncompromising stance on the habitability of the Cubist house. The majority of architects in this book might choose to echo certain elements of previous houses, but each one compromises the purity of the historical original by attempting to meet the requirements of the family/client involved. Ogawa appears to accept no such restrictions, reworking Miesian structural logic even if the client is left in a scarcely habitable house, without privacy or solar protection.

Office of Metropolitan Architecture

Villa dall'Ava

St Cloud, Paris, France, 1984–91

Surely there is a contradiction: the Office of Metropolitan Architecture constantly emphasizes that the lessons of late twentieth-century urbanity inform its philosophy, even providing it with its name; yet the Villa dall'Ava sits comfortably in a Parisian suburb. Has OMA compromised its architecture to fit into this particular part of a city?

The publication of *Delirious New York* in 1978, a book written by founding partner and Dutch architect Rem Koolhaas, did for the American city what Jack Kerouac had achieved for the American highway 20 years earlier. The once banal became immediately acceptable . Koolhaas' message was urban, not the shining towers of inner-city revivalism, but the vacant car lots and contextless wastes around American cities. Suddenly, the network of roads or gridlock of swimming pools illustrated in the book carried equal intellectual weight to a Nolli map of Rome.

The Villa dall'Ava enjoys the sophistication of this intellectual debate. However, the reasons for the success of the house, or even many of OMA's public buildings, are not those of the practice's predominant philosophy. For Koolhaas' urban vision, though based on American models, had a source closer to home, as the situation already existed in the Netherlands. The proximity of Amsterdam and Rotterdam has turned the southern Netherlands, the Randstaad, into a megalopolis – the Dutch 'Los Angeles' – united by a

An uncompromising attitude is taken by OMA in the design of the Villa dall'Ava, where the customary pitched roof and chocolate-box style of the suburban house is replaced by the tougher, more cosmopolitan ideals of steel and glass.

The kitchen is partitioned from the sitting room by a gently curving wall. Nothing is allowed to break the link between the interior of the house and the garden outside.

This section, taken through the swimming pool, reveals the sheer luxury of a house in which such a feature can be so easily accommodated.

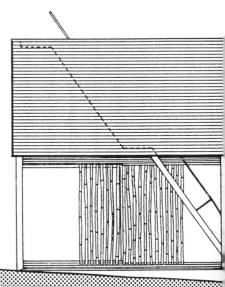

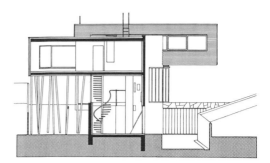

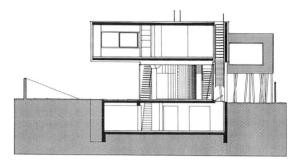

OMA has fully exploited the narrow suburban plot with its gradual fall across the site. The parents' and child's bedrooms are placed at a discreet distance from each other, separated by the living room, as can be seen in these sections.

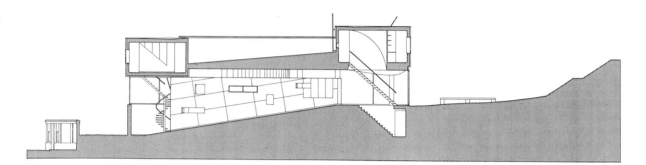

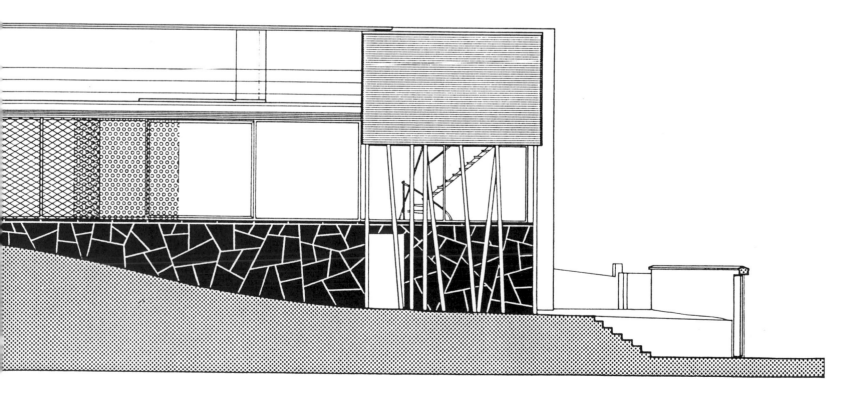

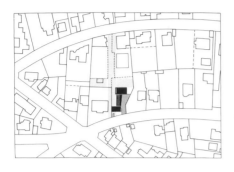

Neighbours and the planning authorities were initially aghast at the prospect of such a building within their bourgeois midst. Yet eventually good architecture won.

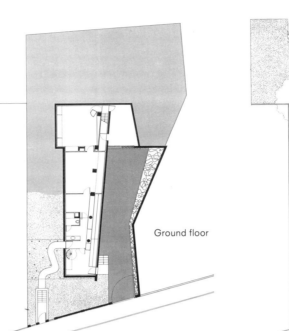

Ground floor

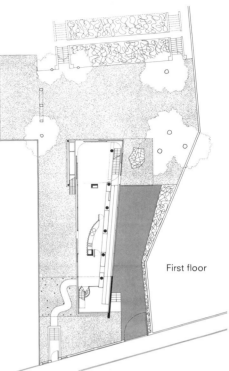

First floor

constant timetable of trains and a network of bicycle lanes containing no cities, only towns.

OMA's place in Dutch architectural history rests on its being the first post-war Dutch practice to make the break with the Netherlands' almost seamless links back to the heroic period of modernism. The practice departs from the international style, turning, instead, to a reworking of Mies van der Rohe or Richard Neutra. Others, such as Stéphane Beel (see page 79) and Xaveer de Geyter (see page 162), have followed, forming, in the process, a whole new axis of architects exploring structure. The Villa dall'Ava, therefore, does confront its suburban environment but with the panache of American structural forms.

The specific references start with an irony. The series of Case Study Houses built in Los Angeles from 1945 were the inspiration of John Entenza, editor and publisher of *Arts & Architecture*. Similarly, the client of the Villa dall'Ava is the publisher of many of France's leading architectural magazines, such as *Le Moniteur*. The two men were more than aware of the possibilities of good buildings (what better way to annoy your competitors than to commission a house so good that even they are forced to publish it?), encouraging a more liberal attitude to architectural experimentation than an average client.

OMA's interests, however, were exactly right for the site, a gently sloping plot squeezed between the high walls of neighbouring gardens. The familiar Paris skyline would be visible if you could rise above the walls and vegetation of the neighbours' gardens. Another house by OMA, a villa in Kralingen, Rotterdam (1989), deals with similar problems, as it is positioned against a dyke. The solution, that time, was to place bedrooms in a masonry block at the lower level and float the living room of steel and glass over the top of both bedrooms and dyke. This organization made the most of the views and allowed OMA to play off solids against the transparent structure. The garden elevation makes reference to a Miesian pavilion, though the lower street façade, with its

An alternative to the leisurely ramped corridor, this spiral staircase provides access to the living room and then continues up to the child's bedroom.

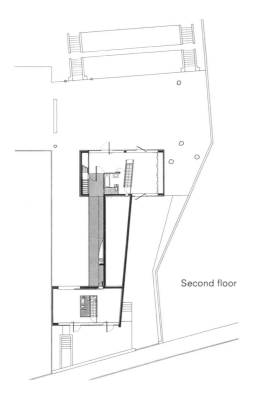

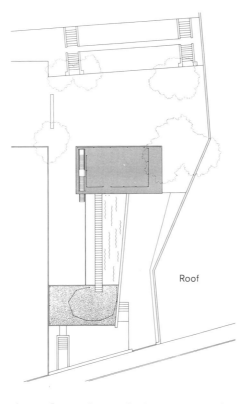

Second floor

Roof

Floor plans (from left to right): ground floor, entrance and utilities; first floor, living room and kitchen; second floor, parents' and child's bedrooms; roof, swimming pool.

strip windows, looks like something out of a Dutch architectural guidebook.

The Villa dall'Ava responds to its site in a deliberately more reckless form – a minimal glass pavilion with an *in situ* concrete box on top. The ground-floor living room is therefore set firmly in the garden with parents' and daughter's bedrooms placed above, benefitting from the view. But how can concrete be supported by glass? Such an inversion of logic organizes the plan while characterizing the architecture as something of an experiment in structure very different from the neat abstract geometry of the usual Dutch domestic architecture. The master bedroom cantilevers over the basement garage; the daughter's bedroom goes one step better and is raised on irregularly angled columns. Both bedrooms are clad in corrugated aluminium, rather than the typical Dutch render, a material common to OMA, but one first explored by Gerrit Rietveld in the garage and chauffeur's quarters of a house in Utrecht (1928).

A hierarchy of spaces, from public to semi-private to private, characterizes the interior. A concrete path winds its way through the forest of columns, dropping visitors off at a deliberately underplayed door which leads into a voluminous entrance hall. A double-height vestibule has a ramp rising steadily up to the living room, and a staircase spirals up to the daughter's bedroom two

floors above. The living room, though open plan, is broken down into three parts: a dining area back towards the entrance hall, a sitting area out towards the garden, and a kitchen, partitioned with profiled polyester screens, in between. The room also widens in the middle, converting the more intimate activities of dining into the more relaxed nature of a sitting room.

Stairs lead up to the parents' bedroom. But more exciting is a second set of stairs, partially outside, leading people up to a rooftop swimming pool. OMA has attempted to keep the roof as flat as the water's surface. There are no handrails, no ledges, no convenient balustrades: only two Astroturfed roofs to greet either end of a lap and the view over Paris. The pool can be placed within OMA's urban tradition both graphically as part of a collage straight out of *Delirious New York* and ideologically as a symbol of the fragmentation of contemporary city life. Both are correct, though the pool's elevation high over Paris also acknowledges, but updates, the imagery of Case Study House #22 by Pierre Koenig, photographed by Julius Schulman, cantilevered over Los Angeles.

Gerrit Rietveld first explored corrugated aluminium in the garage and chauffeur's quarters of a house at Utrecht (1928).

Chapter 3

Organic houses

Frank Lloyd Wright, Barnsdall house, Los Angeles, California, 1921.

The word organic has been used most indiscriminately to describe architecture. For some, it refers to those buildings that spurn the rational ideals of architecture in favour of more zoomorphic forms. For others, it is an insistence on buildings that respond, if not reflect, the context of their location and programme. For a few, it goes further, embracing and absorbing naturally inspired decoration. But organic can remain an essential work tool of the architecture critic if it is restricted to two definitions, as in this chapter; a counterweight to the neglect of context by pure white modernists and an individualism opposed to the sometimes anonymous geometry of Miesian pavilions.

American architect Louis Sullivan (1856–1924) thought that the essence of every problem contains and suggests its own solution,[1] justifying a later generation of organic architects who saw final form as latent or already in existence. Frank Lloyd Wright (1867–1959), first employed by Sullivan, went further, arguing that each part of a building should have an identity which adds up to a whole. The range of houses and buildings by Wright crosses the entire spectrum of organic architecture.

The rigidity of Wright's earliest domestic works, such as the Charnley (1892) and Blossom (1892) Houses, was merely the expression of a still-immature architect; their lack of originality was swiftly replaced by the iconoclastic Prairie Houses.

The Robie house (1909), for example, departed from the nineteenth century's fetishistic division of rooms to provide a freer ground plan where parallel rooms became interpenetrating volumes. Wright's first houses were placed in simple suburbs. His later houses, such as Fallingwater (1935) and Taliesin West (1938), dealt with steep, rural slopes or the desert.[2]

Wright's solutions showed how architecture could be part of the landscape, expressed, though, as a sophisticated section and plan. That lesson has certainly not been ignored. Scogin Elam & Bray's Chmar house (see page 176) is placed in a forest, fitting into a clearing created by a fallen tree. Yet, the Chmar house, for all its ease in its surroundings, does not ignore the challenge of an interior and exterior where rooms, circulation and façades achieve a complexity that satisfies its owners. And Sergio Puente and Ada Dewes' jungle house (see page 144) is placed over a stream with the same kind of symbolic power, though less grand, as Wright's Fallingwater.

Other contemporary architects have seen context as so important as to sacrifice their more familiar interests. Barrie Marshall's practice, Denton Corker Marshall, is well-known for its use of forbidding concrete in its more usual city buildings. But Marshall's beach house (see page 120) is largely covered by an embankment of grass, hiding much of the house from view. Xaveer de Geyter, whose

Antoni Gaudí, Casa Batlló, Barcelona, 1905-7.

construction technique places him more logically in chapter 2, sacrifices his more usual approach in the house outside Antwerp (see page 166) where a sand dune dictates the nature of the house just like the boulders and hillside define Fallingwater (see page 107).

Wright also taught architects another lesson about the individuality of buildings. Henry Russell Hitchcock condemned Wright's life as a career that did not advance but fluctuated between abstract and decorative periods.[3] Ironically, after a tour of Europe in 1909 where his Prairie House style influenced even Mies, Wright returned home to develop his architecture into a more decorative phase, producing buildings such as the Barnsdall House (1921) with its parallel volumes set on end and its references to ethnic art. Wright was to revert to purer forms in the 1930s but, after the second world war, his passion for decoration returned with the Gammage Memorial Auditorium in Arizona (1956), and his enthusiasm for unorthodox volumes can be seen in the spiral floor plan of the Guggenheim Museum (1959).

These more decorative phases have become one of the strongest elements in Wright's legacy to his country. Bruce Goff (1904–82), described by Mark Alden Branch as 'a Wright admirer who took Wright's ideas in aesthetic directions Wright never pursued',[4] imaginatively explored three-dimensional geometry, 'using circles, triangles, stars and (in the well-known Bavinger house of 1950) logarithmic spirals as ordering devices'.[5] Goff also turned to unorthodox materials, such as coal, glass and carpet stretching up walls. Goff bred a whole generation of American architects like Bart Prince (see page 148), who followed Goff's forms and aesthetics.

Europe, meanwhile, developed its own routes to organic architecture. First came decoration, not one referring to the vulgarity of the nineteenth century's Gothic Revival styles but one inspired by something more natural. The strangely shaped façades and mixture of colourful tiles of Antoni Gaudí (1852–1926) and apartment blocks and houses in Barcelona such as Palau Güell (1889) or the Casa Batlló (1905–7) went way beyond an eccentric, regionalist form of art nouveau.

Second came the development of an almost sculptural architecture. Hugo Häring's (1882–1958) work, such as the main railway station for Leipzig and the Garkau farm buildings, both from the 1920s, provided a visual reference for his 'organ-like' architecture, declaring that, to discover form, architects must be in harmony with nature.[6] Häring never built much though Hans Scharoun (1893–1972), highly influenced by him, did. The curved forms of Scharoun's house for the Weißenhofsiedlung in Stuttgart (1927) contrast markedly with the rigidity of Le Corbusier's villas or Mies' apartment blocks on the same site.

Frank Lloyd Wright, Robie
house, Chicago, 1908 (above,
right). Frank Lloyd Wright,
Taliesin West, Scottsdale,
Arizona, 1938 (below).

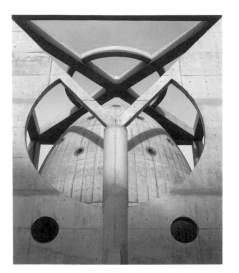

Masaharu Takasaki, Zero Cosmology, Kagoshima, Kyushu, 1989-91 (right). Hans Scharoun, Schminke house, Löbau, Saxony, 1933 (below).

Scharoun continued to develop this form in the 1930s with a series of houses, such as the Schminke House (1933) with its irregular floor plans expressed as a series of cantilevered terraces, which rejected his peers' predetermined geometric forms. Scharoun's skill was to blend the non-decorative purity of pure white modernism with the kind of freedom encouraged by Wright. The inspiration can be seen in Ushida Findlay's Truss Wall house (see page 193), where the form of construction allows for an extraordinary fluidity. Masaharu Takasaki's Zero Cosmology (see page 136) does likewise, forcing concrete into highly symbolic shapes.

What unites both American and European organic architecture, however, is the folk-tale, that very nineteenth-century interest in the often macabre. Gaudí was in contact with the darker, animistic side of human nature, an aspiration shared with other arts such as Wagner's music or Rousseau's paintings. Wright and his followers absorbed something of the American equivalent. 'What Prince has done, like Jefferson and Wright and Goff before him is to transform certain common, vernacular conditions of American culture into an idealized, classical, architectural expression,' says Christopher Mead.[7] Wright's could be taken as the idealized, American, suburban home. Prince has transformed the American shingle style into the anthropomorphic shapes of the Price House or his own home (see page 151).

Bart Prince, house, Albuquerque, New Mexico, 1983-84.

The folk-tale still inspires the work of other contemporary architects. Take Herman Melville's short story, 'I and my chimney':[8] a man builds his house dominated by a chimney, 12 feet square at the base and 4 feet square at the top. The chimney makes him feel at home since it does not talk back like his wife. The chimney is also a tyrant, however, forcing him and his wife to walk around the perimeter of the house, creating a confusion of rooms, each of a peculiar scale, some as passages to another room and some with nine doors. 'Almost every room, like a philosophical system was in itself an entry, or passageway to other rooms and systems, a whole suite of entries, in fact.'

This image could be a description of the work of Frank Gehry (see page 129) or Josh Schweitzer (see page 112). Gehry's early houses, such as his own in Santa Monica (1978), looked to the local vernacular for inspiration, just like Wright, but one based on the aggressive reality of late twentieth-century urban America. His later houses such as the Winton Guest House (1987) and the Schnabel House (1989), however, seek a sculptural architecture of abstract forms rising from a free ground-floor plan taken as a statement on the American suburb. The shapes – squares, oblongs and even cones – make a house where rooms and passageways are all different proportions, creating a profile not too distant from Melville's imaginary chimney. Schweitzer's Monument is an even better

comparison (see page 118), where each feature appears almost like a child's caricature of a folkloric home.

Gehry and Schweitzer, via an updated interpretation of the vernacular, complete the circle of organic architecture. Both achieve the two stated aims of organicism; a counterweight to the neglect of context by pure white modernists, and an individualism opposed to the sometimes anonymous geometry of the Miesian pavilion.

1. Sullivan, Louis. 'The tall office building artistically considered', in *Kindergarten chats and other writings*. New York, 1947.

2. Haragughi, Hideaki. *A comparative analysis of 20th century houses*. London: Academy Editions, 1989.

3. Hitchcock, Henry Russell. *Modern architecture: romanticism and reintegration*. New York: Payson and Clarke, 1929.

4. Branch, Mark Alden. 'A breed apart'. *Progressive Architecture*, June 1992.

5. Ibid.

6. Häring, Hugo. *Schriften, Entwerfe, Bauten*. Stuttgart: 1965.

7. Mead, Christopher. *Houses by Bart Prince*. Albuquerque: University of New Mexico Press, 1991.

8. Melville, Herman. 'I and my chimney'. *Pierre, Israel Potter, the confidence man, tales and Billy Budd*. New York: The Library of America, 1984.

Joshua Schweitzer
The Monument

Joshua Tree, California, USA, 1988–90

At first glance, the Monument would seem to have more to connect it to the architecture of Frank Gehry than to that of Frank Lloyd Wright. The three principal rooms do not flow freely into one another, but quite the opposite. The house is a compilation of one-room buildings, a principle worked up by Gehry. But Wright's contribution to domestic architecture went way beyond one simple idea. His organicism plugged into an American architectural tradition of mysticism to which Joshua Schweitzer's house is also allied.

Schweitzer comes from Kansas, a fact relevant only because his home state appears to have influenced him in two ways. First, there is his all-American upbringing. Schweitzer, born in the 1950s, sees himself as belonging to the first television generation whose heroes appeared in shows such as the *Flintstones* and the *Jetsons*. Such cartoon visuals inspired a faux-Neolithic, rather crude response to form, termed 'New primitivism'. Whereas Wright might have turned to the fashionable imagery of his time, such as the Mayan motifs of the Barnsdall House (1921), Schweitzer tuned into the television equivalent.

The second factor is the great outdoors. Schweitzer built and lived in a tepee in 1972. Naturally, the space inside was far taller than it was wide. Such cheeky perversion of the traditional domestic scale has stayed with him, reaching into his habitually reversed ratios of width to height

Like the set of a Hollywood movie, the Monument stands in the middle of the desert. Yet instead of the OK Corall, Josh Schweitzer suggests the sophistication and culture of contemporary Los Angeles. The powerful impact is achieved using cheap materials – Gyproc board cut to size, covered in stucco and then painted.

The strong colours chosen by Schweitzer, despite their lack of contextualism, confront the desert in a suitably strong manner. After all, this house is concerned with creating a strongly organic image but one which is far more abstract than the Gothic fantasies of Gaudí or Goff.

and often asymmetrical windows and oversized doors. This Alice-in-Wonderland world neatly fits into Anthony Vidler's update of the Gothic. Indeed, the main character's house in Melville's story of 'I and my chimney', cited in Vidler's *The architectural uncanny*, has a chimney '12 feet at the base and 4 feet wide at the top'. The chimney dominates the interior, forcing rooms into a labyrinth of corridors around the central feature. The story, so Gothic in its imagery, traces Schweitzer's architecture back to Wright's organicism.

Perhaps it was the shape of the tepee that got Schweitzer noticed by Gehry. Schweitzer got a job with him in 1984, just as the office was beginning to build what had earlier been only ideas. Gehry's theoretical Tract house (1981), a paradigm of the American lifestyle, had broken down the typical suburban house into a nine-part grid where each block was a house in its own right. Gehry was beginning to liberate form from function, producing fragmented compositions of abstract geometry and breaking down buildings into more than one object. It was just a short step from Gehry's Tract house to the Winton house's (see page 129) collection of one-room buildings. Schweitzer's tepee could easily have been the original for the chimney-shaped entrance of the Winton house or the copper-clad columns of the later Schnabel house (1989). How gratifying for any young architect to have his early ideas

Inside, no two rooms are the same. Thus the living room (opposite) is accommodated within its own block – a voluminous, double-height space on which only a sleeping deck impinges. There is also a comfortable balance between the necessary ease of a weekend home and the formality of Los Angeles' high-culture artefacts (right).

Ground floor plan. Rooms are connected to one another in an L-shaped plan, although, in reality, each room is marked out by its own volume and colour.

The cut-outs, which on the exterior look like part of the scenery, provide views of the desert, carefully edited by Schweitzer.

of form and scale legitimized by a celebrity.

Schweitzer did not stay with Gehry's office for long. Much of his early work was building refurbishment, although it was in a strange way related to some of the themes of his past. There is his own house, an old swimming school, where three existing buildings, each one an essential part of his home, sit separated around a vast swimming pool. And there is his work on the restoration of the Samuels-Navarro house (1928) by Frank Lloyd Wright in Los Angeles for actress Diane Keaton. But the Monument, for four friends and himself, was the new-build project that allowed Schweitzer to develop those early influences into a homogenous whole.

The apparently barren location is somewhat misleading. The Joshua Tree national park is high desert full of magnificent rocks. The never-ending growth of Los Angeles, though more than three hours' drive away, has turned much of the surrounding areas into nascent suburbs of tract houses catching up with vast shopping malls. Schweitzer's house is not so much a comment on as a commitment to an area where man-made insertions compare so badly with the wild.

After all, the building is far from expensive. Common Gyproc board has been cut down to size, covered in stucco and punctured with redwood window frames. The three principal rooms are linked in an L-shape, but each one is a separate and different-coloured volume: the outdoor room is orange, the living room green and the bedroom blue.

The materials and colours give the house a two-dimensional appearance – like a stage set, perhaps, in one of Schweitzer's favourite cartoons. For the Monument, paradoxically, has a certain nightmarish, though friendly, quality, just like a Melville short story. Asymmetrical doors and windows read as scars or features on a face; inside, the weird openings exaggerate the peculiarity of the interiors where spaces are, of course, of Schweitzer's preferred dimensions.

Schweitzer makes little attempt to tone his building down to the colour of its dusty surroundings, challenging the more landscape-based architectural approach of Antoine Predock, for example (see page 50). But the house does sit easily, surrounded by the rocks. It could be read as an abstraction of the desert rocks, fulfilling Wright's concept of houses fitting into, not on, the landscape. But such an interpretation is too easy. The Monument is at one with nature, but has been developed in a somewhat more figurative, even abstract, aesthetic than the Gothic fantasies of Bruce Goff or Bart Prince (see page 151). Organic it may be, but of its own time.

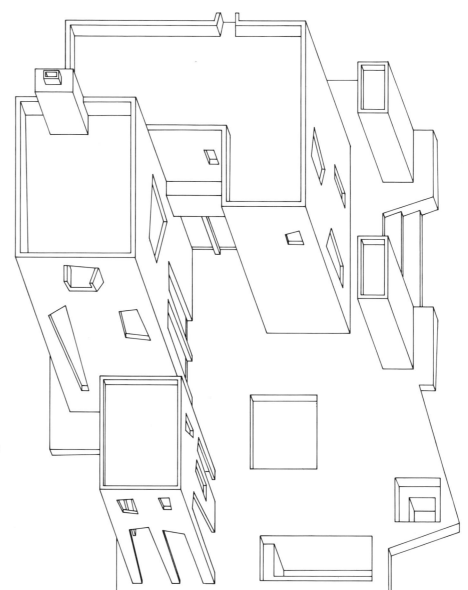

Like Gehry or Wright, Schweitzer organizes the interior on the principle of dispersal, pushing each element until a room becomes almost a building in its own right. The section (below) shows how each room is given its own identity by its particular volumetric shape.

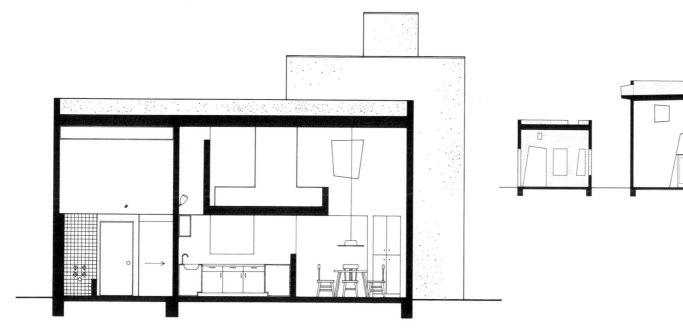

Barrie Marshall, Denton Corker Marshall

Cowes house

Phillip Island, Victoria, Australia, 1984–94

If Frank Lloyd Wright's Fallingwater (see page 107) fulfils the criterion of a house absolutely dependent on its location for its final form, then Barrie Marshall, partner of Denton Corker Marshall, has achieved much the same ambition but with a different result. His beach house slips into its ocean-side setting so successfully that the plan, section and elevations would be redundant in any other context.

Kitty Miller's Bay is the only one on the south side of Phillip Island protected from the ocean swell. Sand dunes, covered in native grasses, hug the shore and run up to two headlands which frame the bay. Marshall has been skin-diving and spearfishing off the bay ever since he was young: 'I always thought, what a great place to live.' Three ungainly houses have now been built around the bay, with other scruffy ones on the access road stretching away from the sea. Marshall, though, still feels some of the city-dweller's guilt about having a house there. 'What if someone did get to built; how would I have felt if some big number had gone up?

'I decided, no matter what, that the wrong thing to do was to make the house an object; no matter how fine, how elegant, how cleverly executed – such as a butterfly perched on the crest of a dune – it would have been the wrong thing to do,' he says. Marshall decided, instead, to 'deform architecture' so that the appearance of the house is like an 'abstract sculpture' or 'non-event'. Such context was generated by the site.

Anyone approaching the house drives along the road from the north, and is usually unimpressed by the scruffy buildings and swampy land. 'You forget the dismal drive' on arrival, however, with the magnificent view of the bay. Marshall did not want his house to add to the existing clutter of buildings, nor did he want it to impose when viewed from the sea. The location, therefore, created a natural front and back to the house, emphasized by the desired views from the house – plenty of the sea, none towards the rear. Unfortunately, such a straightforward orientation was complicated by the sun, shining from the rear, and the winds – cooling off the sea in the summer, unpleasantly cold off the land in the winter.

At first, Marshall had considered some sort of timber construction, but he then decided that this would not work. Then, 'I wanted the house to feel like part of the earth, a cave, both inside and out.' Two elements, both in black pigmented *in situ* concrete, were created, one a skewed parallelogram 50 metre x 4 metre (164 feet x 13 feet, 1 inch) and the other a 4 metre (13 feet, 1 inch) high wall around four sides of a courtyard. The south wall of the courtyard is the rear façade of the house, the north is entirely blank, the east has a small break to allow cars through, and the west has three garages. The house takes up the space between the

Despite the urban, man-made nature of concrete, the appearance of Marshall's beach house has been softened by the creation of a dune that rises and merges with the naturally occurring dunes all around.

At one with its surroundings, the Cowes house blends into the dune on which it stands.

The house is a linear
arrangement of rooms
squeezed between two
elements: the parallelogram
and the four walls of the
courtyard. The first wall is
blank, the second contains the
garages, the third is broken to
allow cars through and the
fourth provides windows.

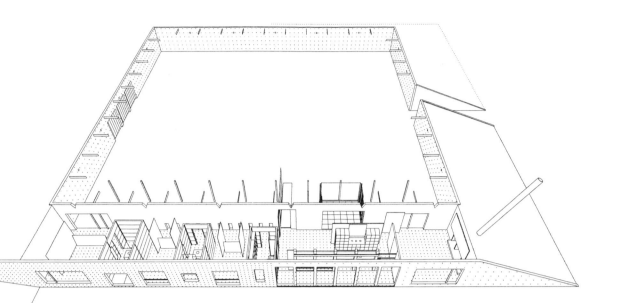

parallelogram and the courtyard. New, man-made
dunes were extended over the roof of the house
and banked up against the walls at a 30° angle.
From the land, it seems as though the building no
longer exists. From the sea, it has become 'a wall, a
piece of cliff, a slash of rock-face into the dunes'.

Once Marshall had taken that step, the rest of
the problems seemed to be solved. The interior is
subdivided into a series of 'temporary resting
places' – Marshall is keen not to refer to them as
rooms. This notion seems appropriate for a house
where people come from the beach and just dump
down their towels, but the resting places are far
from simple. Each room has a view of the sea from
windows whose height is set according to the
activity inside: low sills for views from beds, higher
sills for privacy in bathrooms. The result is
consistent with modernist notions of an exterior
expressing interior volumes.

The ocean-side façade becomes a dense wall
punctured with windows. In contrast, the
courtyard façade has few such openings. The
master bedroom and living room fully occupy
either end of the house, and have windows on
either side and small slots at knee height – what
Marshall's partner John Denton calls 'penguin
windows' – illuminating the passageway behind
the bedrooms. The almost-blank façade protects
the house from the north wind and the extreme
sun of the summer. The orientation also makes the

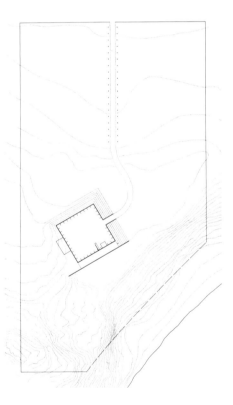

Site plan. The house is
reached down a long lane
and on into the sand dunes
beside the sea.

Rooms are left intentionally sparse inside, reflecting a lifestyle of beach towels thrown on the floor and the constant accumulation of sand.

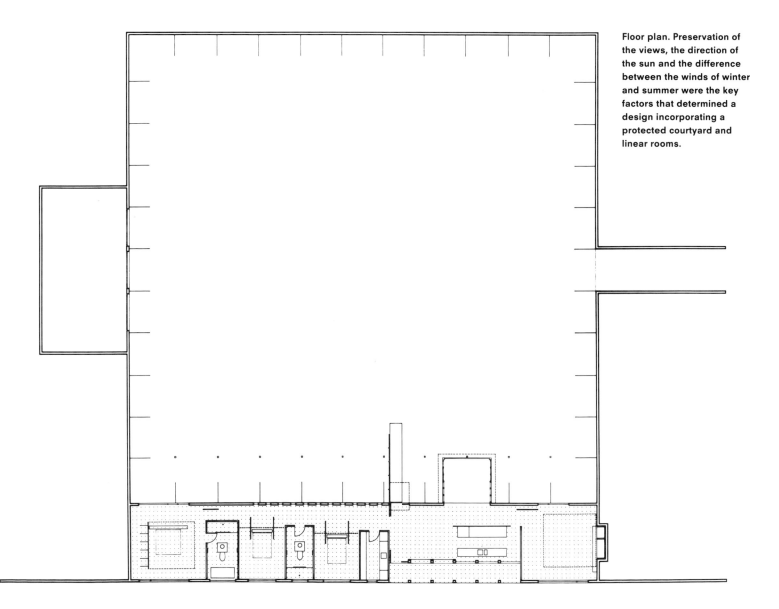

Floor plan. Preservation of the views, the direction of the sun and the difference between the winds of winter and summer were the key factors that determined a design incorporating a protected courtyard and linear rooms.

The entrance is emphasized by a screen of steel (far left). Big windows (left) face the sea, though this is only possible because the seaward side is the south and shaded side.

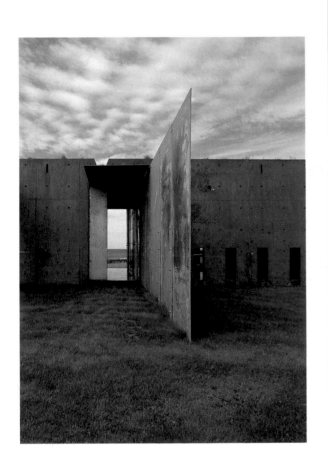

The walls and dunes around the courtyard are broken only once where two triangular-shaped retaining walls allow cars to enter. Even this simple device adds to Marshall's assemblage of abstract elements in the landscape.

The two façades of the house:
the skewed parallelogram
facing the sea (top) and one
of the four walls of the
courtyard (bottom), which is
incised with windows unlike
the other three.

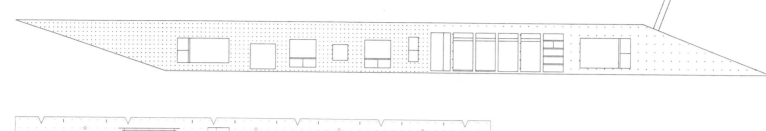

courtyard essential to the building's composition.

Daryl Jackson's courtyard at Bermagui (see page 86) is something of a focus for the activities of the house. Marshall's, in contrast, plays that and a different role. The courtyard has certain practical reasons: 'There is no back yard (in the country read junk yard), so all the rubbish you collect' is hidden away in the garages, but there are also more abstract notions. The courtyard walls obscure all views of the sea, making those from the house all the more precious. Marshall also sees the courtyard as something of an oasis or 'cultivated precinct', to be compared to the kitchen gardens of outback homesteads.

Marshall does achieve a house intimately connected with its location, but one that is expressed firmly within the language of elsewhere. His concern with context, for example, contrasts with the locals' lack of it. The black pigmented concrete, steel panels and terrazzo of the interior have much more to do with Denton Corker Marshall's architectural vocabulary than the clichéd timber of weekend cottages. He also subverts the idyllic notion of home, comparing his own beach house to Man Ray's photographs of the 1920s and 1930s not for his surrealism but for his 'transformation of expectations, where the ordinary is seen as new not because of any stylistic or technical contrivance, but as transformation through another way of looking'.

The dining room, with its floor-to-ceiling windows with views of the sea beyond, is an example of the formal aspect of the house.

Frank Gehry
Winton guest house

Wayzata, Minnesota, USA, 1983–87

From the Hoffmann house (1967) to the Ackerberg house 20 years later (see page 36), Richard Meier's architecture has been a great constant. Frank Gehry's work shows no such evenness. A series of houses in the 1980s, like the Winton guest house, seems strangely dislocated from earlier work and, more surprisingly, quite distinct from his contemporaneous public commissions.

The differences are readily apparent. The Winton guest house, like the earlier Sirmai-Peterson house (1986) and the later Schnabel house (1989), is a collection of one-room buildings, whose various shapes and finishes add up to a frankly sculptural composition. Gehry's own house in Santa Monica (1978), in contrast, is an addition to a traditional cottage whose assumed disorder in plan and use of gritty materials clearly prefigures his Norton house on Venice Beach, the Loyola Law School or his Aerospace Museum in Los Angeles, all of them completed in the 1980s. But how great is the gap between the two styles?

Gehry plugs into the many architectural rules of Frank Lloyd Wright. Buildings should be objects set in their landscape. Such contextual aspirations are

The Winton guest house is an assembly of one-room elements, each with its own form and clad in its own particular material, building up into a sculptural whole.

The Winton guest house is one of a series of houses by Frank Gehry, which includes the Schnabel house (right) and the Norton house (far right).

Each room is a building in its own right. Here, the garage stands in front of the two guest bedrooms, while at the core rises the chimney-like living room.

readily available in a city such as Los Angeles. His own house and the Norton house are robust and harsh answers to the late twentieth-century urban environment. The suburbs, though, offer few clues. Gehry's answer is the architecture of the mysterious shapes of the Winton guest house. If the city encourages an architecture that predicts an anarchic future, then the American suburb encourages what Anthony Vidler calls the 'uncanny'.

Wright's architecture also called for a 'breaking of the box' – a floor plan that reduced the complexity of nineteenth-century living arrangements to the open-plan ideal. Gehry develops such a maxim to a late twentieth-century extreme. The Norton house (1983), with its famous study – a pod like a lifeguard tower, separate from the house and overlooking the sea – does just that. But Gehry's reasoning behind the dispersal of the Winton and Schnabel houses attempts not only to liberate one family but to act as a critique on society as a whole.

The houses of the 1980s are direct descendants of Gehry's experimental Tract house (1981). The starting-point of his project was Denise Scott Brown's *Levittown*, a reappraisal of the American suburb as a decent place that had been transformed into repetitive tract housing by the neglect of architects. Gehry took the argument further, splitting his Tract house into a grid of nine parts where each room stood as a different-shaped

In treating each room as though it were a separate building within a village, the Tract house (1981) is an experimental precursor to the Winton guest, Norton and Schnabel houses.

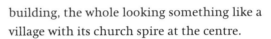

Gehry develops many of Frank Lloyd Wright's architectural rules. The plan of the Winton guest house shows him 'breaking the box' of nineteenth-century house plans and spinning individual rooms away from a central space.

building, the whole looking something like a village with its church spire at the centre.

The idea, developed in the unbuilt Smith house (1981), allowed Gehry to separate form from function. Gehry could develop architecture not as one entity, but as a far richer series of ideas or abstract shapes. And his clients, especially the more intense domestic kind, were given more with which they could identify. As Gehry says: 'Those images can relate to all kinds of symbolic things: ideas you have liked, places you have liked, bits and pieces of your life that you would like to recall.' The Tract house conveniently also tied into Gehry's other passion, material.

Scott Brown continues her argument by pointing out that the early modern movement was obsessed with housing, seeing technology as the way to mass production. Nowadays, the American suburb is little more than images from a cheap building catalogue. Gehry disagrees. His own house has an intentionally provisional air, with its chain-mail fence and corrugated-iron panels. 'I like the unfinished,' he says, seeing beauty in the character of a production process so often lost in technical manufacturing.

Yet, such an aesthetic, no doubt suitable for Santa Monica or Venice Beach, has little relevance to the aspirations of a rich suburban client. Instead, Gehry has sought to clad his shapes in a variety of luxurious materials, such as the lead-

The abstract, evocative interiors of the Winton guest house rise from a free ground-floor plan. Here, for example, is the apex of the chimney-like living room.

coated copper of the Schnabel house, emphasizing the variety of shapes. But there is still something provisional about the act, with sheet metal clipped to wooden frames like the backdrop to a film set.

Ironically, the Winton guest house is furthest from Gehry's rough-and-ready style. The clients wanted little to do with it, and the harsh climate of Minnesota ensured substantial construction. Otherwise, the house fits neatly into Gehry's domestic agenda. Perhaps the site helped. The Wintons already lived in a Miesian brick box on a heavily wooded lakeside estate, designed by Philip Johnson for Mr and Mrs Richard C. Davis in 1952. The couple loved the house, but were rather short of space whenever their five children or growing number of grandchildren came to stay. But they did not want any new building to ruin or overwhelm what was there.

The Wintons has approached Johnson who informed them that he no longer built houses. They asked Gehry to come and help instead, having read of him in the *New York Times*. The choice of Gehry to extend a Johnson house was not as bizarre as at first it might seem since Gehry has always recognized the importance of Johnson's New Canaan House (1949) in his own development of one-room buildings.

Gehry's response to the Wintons' project is a collection of pure shapes, 'objects-in-a-landscape'

The form of the living room has many different interpretations. They include Wright's ideal of the hearth as the core of any house, which has been exaggerated by Gehry on an almost surreal scale. But there is also Anthony Vidler's concept of the 'uncanny', in which organic architecture is perceived as the realization of the often uncomfortable imagery of the folk-tale.

placed together 'like a Morandi still-life'; a black-painted sheet metal chimney-shaped living room, an unpainted sheet metal sleeping loft, a chimney alcove in the same brick as Johnson's original house, one bedroom covered in limestone, another in black sheets and the kitchen and garage clad in Finnish plywood. The separate shapes build up into an impressive sculpture, an effect emphasized by their location on a slight rise in the grounds with the grass growing right up to the very base of each block.

A sculpture in a garden solved the Wintons' worries; the guest house does not read as a building and, therefore, cannot compete but only contrasts with Johnson's original. Gehry also achieved another of the clients' wishes. The rooms inside enjoy a remarkable degree of openness with the flow of rooms into one another and the windows providing views of parts of the house. And yet there is still a sense of adventure; the sitting room is a vast chimney, the back of the stairs exposes rough carpentry and the sleepingloft could be a tree house. 'It is hoped,' says Gehry, referring to the 'uncanny' scale and proportions of the interior, 'that this building will have a certain amount of humour and mystery and fantasy.'

Masaharu Takasaki
Zero Cosmology

Kagoshima, Kyushu, Japan, 1989–91

Without doubt, Masaharu Takasaki is an organic architect: 'Architecture aims to be a living body in its environment,' he says. The shapes and floor plans of Zero Cosmology reveal the fluidity appropriate to a follower of Bruce Goff. The dramatic living room takes Wright's ideas of the hearth at the core of a home to a somewhat illogical extreme. This is Japan, however, where houses have problems fitting into a city and where an architect like Takasaki has his own non-Western agenda. What kind of a building does this make Zero Cosmology?

The house is made entirely of *in situ* concrete, its shuttering marks left clearly exposed. Such a material seems uncompromising compared with the generous use of wood in Bart Prince's Price house (see page 154), or severely monochrome when contrasted to the colourfulness of Joshua Schweitzer's Monument (see page 118). Yet, concrete does not exclude the house from Takasaki's organic goals. The early modernism of Le Corbusier, for example, sacrificed the true nature of materials so that the hours of craftsmanship necessary to achieve the pure forms were disguised beneath the rhetoric of industrially produced perfection. Post-war brutalism reversed such orthodoxy, leaving concrete to express its inherent organic identity.

Takasaki has a greater problem verifying an organic architecture for the city. 'The architecture itself contains natural energy and stimulates its natural surroundings,' he says. Yet, Zero Cosmology is squeezed on to a typical Japanese urban plot, surrounded by the ugly tiled roofs of its neighbours and not a rural idyll. The context explains Zero Cosmology's introversion. Tadao Ando does much the same with the Kidosaki house (see page 70), using an abridged version of the outside in a central private courtyard as an alternative to real life. Takasaki goes further still, confining everyday experience purely to the activities of domestic life.

That decision would seem somewhat dictatorial but then Takasaki does claim for himself the grand aim of 'giving birth to a new culture and a new consciousness'. For him, organic architecture is not

Another Japanese house confronts the dull, urban reality of many of the country's cities. In contrast to Eisaku Ushida, Kathryn Findlay or Tadao Ando, however, Zero Cosmology unashamedly embraces the holistic characteristics of Japanese culture. For example the architect looked to the nearby volcano of Sakurajima (below, left) for inspiration in more than just the name.

Crystal Light, an earlier Takasaki house, contains three floors of accommodation around a central courtyard.

The living room lies at the core of the building (opposite), its importance as a place of refuge symbolized by its ovoid shape.

simply about putting people closer to nature through a building but is about introducing humans to a wider spiritual world: 'The force of architecture is its spiritual diversion; only this can induce people to meditate and thus reach a liberated state of mind.' An earlier era would have labelled Takasaki's goal that of abstraction.

The pure geometry of early modern houses, for example, was a direct transference of the abstraction of painting into architecture. People were to be conscious of something other than merely the built form. Yet, Takasaki has not always understood this. Crystal Light (1987), an earlier house, entered under a huge canopy, has three floors of accommodation around a central courtyard. Takasaki claims that the meaning is generated by 'the ongoing dialogue between the building's spiritual essence and its physical forms'.

Yet, Crystal Light is far from abstract. Verandas overlooking the central courtyard are covered in fish-scale-like metal panels; the canopy resembles the body of a gigantic silkworm about to raise its head and nibble a leaf. The house, far from organic, is an essay in zoomorphic forms far too easily recognized to have any symbolic significance. Abstraction, after all, relies on a type of silence, not the frenzied articulation of Crystal Light.

Takasaki has learned that lesson. Zero Cosmology is a far from literal interpretation of a brief. The clients are a businesswoman, Yoshiko

Masaharu Takasaki confronts the uniformity of suburban Japanese cities. The contrast lies not just in the materials – concrete against tiles – but also in the poetry of abstract forms against the more traditional pitched roof.

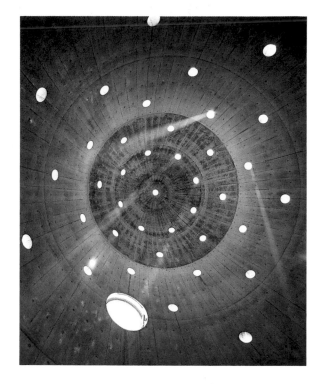

The living room – with various-sized holes punched through its concrete ceiling – achieves an interior which is midway between the simplicity of a Roman bath and the mystery of a modern-day planetarium.

In the stairs between the first and second floors Takasaki's playful geometries in concrete are carried through to those in steel and glass.

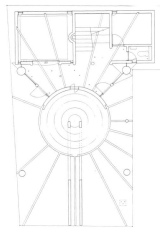
Ground floor

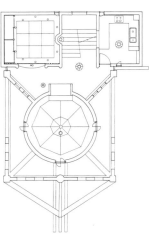
First floor

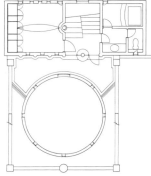
Second floor

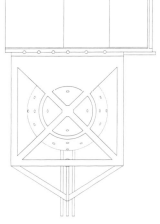
Roof

The base of the ovoid living room hangs, as if unsupported, over a pool of water. The arrangement is certainly extravagant, although strangely democratic since the composition is seen not by the client but rather by any passer-by on the adjacent street.

Hayashiyama, and her daughter, Keiko. The house is located in Kagoshima, the capital city of Kyushu, Japan's largest southern island. The city is dominated by Sakurajima, a still-active volcano. Takasaki has placed the house squarely on a plot surrounded on three sides by roads or lanes. Normal rooms are stacked in pairs on a fourth side against a neighbouring building – the store and music room on the ground floor, Tatami room (a traditional-style living room) and kitchen on the first floor, and bed- and bathroom on the second floor.

The living room, though, differentiates this house and gives it its name. An ovoid volume stands out from the more functional spine of rooms. The living room is supported within an oblong grid of concrete cross-bracings or triangular panels, allowing the curved bottom of the egg to hang apparently unsupported over a shallow pool of water visible from the street. Inside, the room, entered through a circular portal, has no furniture apart from a low row of fitted cupboards with a bench on top. The space enjoys an extraordinary level of light, which enters through 54 openings in one of two sizes, punctured in its walls.

Many might see the living room with its portal as little different from a nuclear shelter mounted above ground, but Takasaki has consciously sought a place of security and privacy for the client. A fairer comparison than a bunker would be with the safe rooms created at the heart of politicians' or

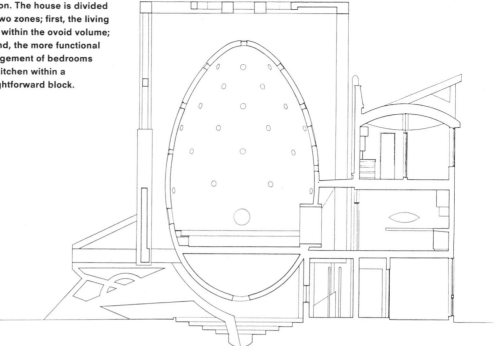

Section. The house is divided into two zones; first, the living room within the ovoid volume; second, the more functional arrangement of bedrooms and kitchen within a straightforward block.

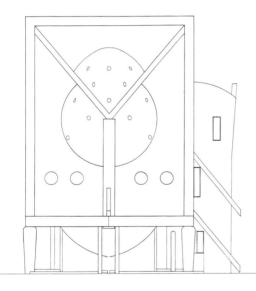

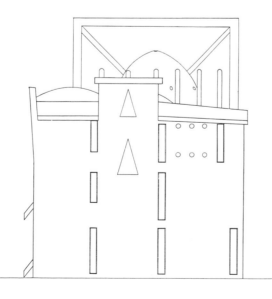

Elevations. The more public façade (above) is dominated by the concrete web in which the ovoid rests; the neighbouring buildings come so close that the back façade (below) is merely a plain wall pierced by simple windows.

businessmen's homes as places of refuge against terrorism. An earlier working title for Zero Cosmology was the Egg house, an obvious comment on the shape of the living room and some of Takasaki's intentions towards that space. Japanese culture sees little of the West's humour in an egg (as in 'egg on your face', for example), preferring, instead, its associations with birth and creativity: for egg, read womb.

Yoshiko Hayashiyama takes this notion further: 'To us the Egg is like a planet, a microcosm for us alone.' Here, Takasaki would agree. Zero Cosmology refers to a place where 'people are incited to realize their views on the Cosmos'. The troubled link between an organic architecture and the city is made good; for Zero Cosmology, sitting below the smoking volcano, 'stimulates its natural surroundings', addressing Sakurajima rather than its crowded urban context.

Ada Dewes and Sergio Puente
La Casa del Ojo de Agua

Santiago Tepetlapa, Mexico, 1985–90

The jungle house has been constructed in two separate parts. A kitchen, dining room and studio are accommodated in one house while, lower down the slope, there is a single house/room for sleeping in. The simple block contains many references – the flight of steps (left) recalls Aztec temples while the doorway (right) is a reminder of a Spanish colonial church door.

The relationship between a babbling stream and a house by Ada Dewes and Sergio Puente is not the only element La Casa del Ojo de Agua has in common with Frank Lloyd Wright's Fallingwater. These architects, like Wright, have created a house where the passage of water, far from being a trick, emphasizes the particularity of the building to its context.

Dewes and Puente break with Wright in significant ways, however: for example, in their treatment of volume. Wright designed houses with open ground plans. Contemporary architecture has legitimized a return to an earlier domestic arrangement. Here, each function, such as living/eating/cooking, has its own dedicated area. Or, more dramatically, each function has a building to itself, as in the work of Frank Gehry (see page 132) or Joshua Schweitzer (see page 115).

Dewes and Puente's interest in the individual identity of separate functions is strongest in their San Bernabé house (1986) outside Mexico City. Here, the house is entered between two gatehouse-like blocks, one containing a bathroom, the other a kitchen. The main part of the house, the living room and bedroom, is then accommodated within another block, separated from the first two by a glazed void.

La Casa del Ojo de Agua divides the various domestic functions between two buildings. One, at the top of the site, is a two-storey block with a studio at first-floor level and a kitchen with its patio dining area at ground level. The lower building (the architects call it the 'main house') is somewhat more unusual, with a patio protected from the weather only by the branches of a mango tree. Below lies a single room – a bedroom with an en suite bathroom – enclosed on three sides not by solid walls but by mosquito nets. Dewes and Puente do not turn to geometric shapes or materials, like Gehry, to differentiate their volumes, but rely on their frankly landscape-architectural approach to make the difference.

The site has no flat ground, just the stream gushing from a natural spring at the top. 'It was the environment of a brook which we converted into the environment of a house. Thus, in a sense, we had to substitute the brook.' They refer to the

The bedroom has only one real wall: the other three are mosquito nets so that 'the mist just passes through the room'.

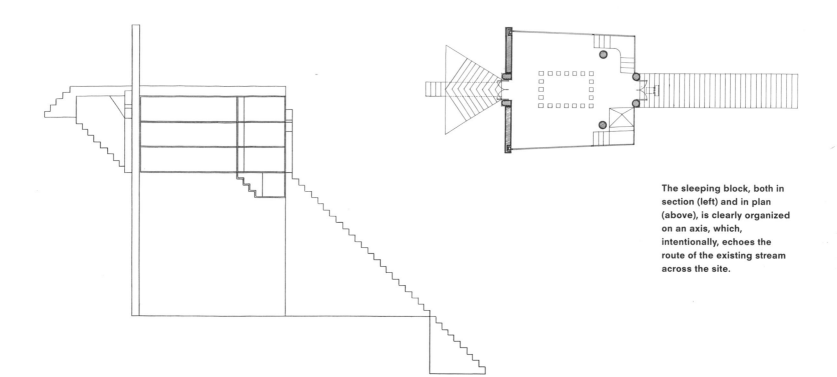

The sleeping block, both in section (left) and in plan (above), is clearly organized on an axis, which, intentionally, echoes the route of the existing stream across the site.

strong *genius loci* of the hillside, creating what they call 'a water architecture' with its 'sunken entrance, a floating room, the flowing out of centres, the running through of circulation'. The obsession with water returns Dewes and Puente to the Wrightian fold (not quite Fallingwater, which hovers above the stream, but certainly the Barnsdall house in Los Angeles [1921] where the water is guided through the house), as they use the route of the stream to unify the disparate blocks.

The flow of water is expressed in one of several forms. The upper house channels the flow under a grill across the floor of the kitchen patio on one side, turning it into a mini-waterfall tumbling into a plunge pool on the other. The stream then continues its journey, passing directly below the lower house before turning into a waterfall shooting into the Atongo river below, just like Fallingwater. The water is constantly visible, with glass bricks on the floor of the lower buildings's bedroom allowing views of the stream as it disappears below the house.

Where La Casa del Ojo de Agua departs from Fallingwater, though not from Wright, is in the nature of its aesthetics. The post-modern world has encouraged a diversity of styles, materials and references to the past that Wright himself only hinted at – he was, after all, a wizard synthesizer of forms. Fallingwater, despite its relationship to the stream and its vertical elements in frestone,

emphasizes the reinforced concrete of its horizontal elements, expressing the uncontextual architecture of cubism and rationalism; the Barnsdall house celebrates the largely Hollywoodesque ethnicity of Mayan art; Taliesin West (1937) recommends an architecture at one with its desert surroundings in both form and situation.

Dewes and Puente carry on a conversation with Mexico and the jungle, but one updated to this era. The architects make references to the historic architecture of Latin America, as does Wright's interest in Mayan culture, or Antoine Predock's early houses (see page 50). The San Bernabé house is laid out on a symmetrical axis and built to a pyramidal section through which the staircase to the upper bedroom rises. The jungle house has some elements consistent with the San Bernabé house, with the symmetrical lower building approached up a steep flight of steps from the river below. Both deliberately recall the Mexican temples of the Aztecs.

As at Frank Lloyd Wright's Fallingwater, the architecture of La Casa del Ojo de Agua is unified by the flow of water through the building.

The San Bernabé house (1986), also by Dewes and Puente, is an earlier indication of the architects' principles: the building is broken down into a series of individual blocks, each one housing a separate function.

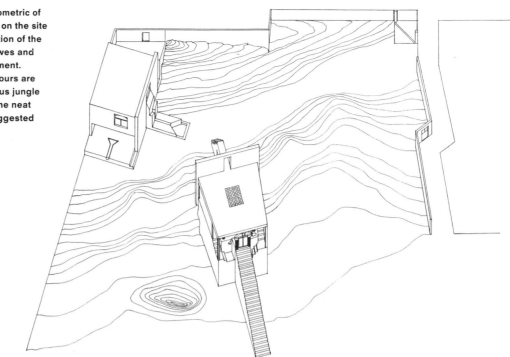

A simplified planometric of the two buildings on the site gives little indication of the true nature of Dewes and Puente's achievement. In reality the contours are covered in a riotous jungle very different to the neat suburban plot suggested in the drawing.

There are other, more recent, historic references. The one solid wall of the lower building is made of sun-dried adobe bricks which were recovered from an old house and have been laid between courses of small pebbles fetched from the nearby river. The shuttered concrete of both front and back portals of the lower house recalls an old Spanish colonial church. And the tiles of the kitchen or their use in the water feature of the upper house are like the decorated pools of Islamic/Iberian architecture, again not dissimilar to Predock's work.

However, Dewes and Puente modernize the experience of living in a way that Wright could never have imagined. Modernism has traditionally sought to turn everyday living into the greatest form of luxury. But the popularity of the outdoors, as seen in inter-war Germany or Britain, and the rise of environmental issues since the second world war have begun to reverse the situation. Now some of the goals of early modern domestic architecture, such as air-conditioning or sufficient garage space, no longer count. Instead, some architects have sought to create houses totally at one with nature; not the neatly packaged view from Scogin Elam & Bray's Chmar house (see page 182), for example, but rather the house as a permanent tent such as Glenn Murcutt's work (see page 225) or Daryl Jackson's vacation house (see page 86).

'We wanted to redefine nature as a force, not as an ornament,' say Dewes and Puente, revealing exactly where they stand. La Casa del Ojo de Agua does little to protect its inhabitants from the jungle, leaving them to experience/enjoy their surroundings with only the minimum of comforts such as running water and electricity. The lower house, for example, is the closest one could get to sleeping outdoors, with only mosquito nets for protection. The architects describe their weekend experiences mystically: 'Sometimes the mist just passes through the room.' Even the shower and toilet/sink are something of an experience, privacy provided only by their relatively sunken position on either side of the back door.

Yet, even the architecture, not only the inhabitants, is exposed to the jungle. 'Rills run and drip and ooze downwards, transforming into juices, slime and moss. Moving stones causes a riot of cochinillas [beetles],' say the architects, their delight almost visible. The inevitable is accepted. 'We chose the materials for their organic qualities and just abandoned them to immediate decay,' they say. Such post-modern perversity reverses what the architects refer to as 'the process of restoration of the old starting a process of decay of the new'.

Bart Prince
Price house

Corona del Mar, California, USA, 1984–89

Wooden shingles are the traditional cladding for US seaside residences. Yet in Bart Prince's hands the traditional becomes the highly unusual starting-point for the Price house.

In reality the forbidding entrance provides protection for the core elements of the house, while the more 'average' elements face the ocean (above and opposite).

Organic architecture, though an exclusive club, has few people who boast of their membership. Bart Prince, for example, claims that his work is autonomous. But his designs for the Price house – practically a definition of organicism with its freeflowing interior spaces, its interlocking geometries, and its use of materials – fit neatly into one historical perspective of American domestic architecture.

That process starts with Frank Lloyd Wright's Prairie houses, which rejected the clutter of the nineteenth-century domestic arrangements in favour of a freeflowing floor plan. The interior was not the floating space of modernism, but one relying on a more visible connection to site and geometry. But it was Bruce Goff who, sticking to Wright's spatial ideals, went on to elaborate that more decorative side of Wright's aesthetics.

The Bavinger house (1950–55) in Oklahoma by Goff became something of an organic icon. Where Wright's houses had emphasized the mythic expansiveness of the US in their strong horizontality, Goff stressed the vertical, recalling an older, folkloric sense of protectiveness. The Bavinger house placed rooms in a spiralling helicoid plan. The interior became a series of spaces, growing naturally out of and into one another.

Goff became the mentor to a whole group of young architects such as Prince, now termed the 'American school'. This phrase, though irritatingly

Inside (opposite), the pod-like living rooms are raised above the cavernous lower level. The expression of the wall as shingle and the pod as timber adds a further decorative element to the interior.

The organic, experimental forms of the O'Brien residence at White Rock, New Mexico (left), and Prince's own house in Albuquerque, New Mexico (below).

geographically imprecise, acknowledges organicism's link to the American vernacular. The individuality of architect and client is constant. But the reliance on shingles, the use of everyday, mass-produced materials in original ways, and the transformation of the average tract plot into a billboard, tie the 'school' firmly to the suburban reality of America with its detached houses.

Prince was firmly linked to this world. He had attended Arizona State University in the late 1960s, ploughing a largely anonymous course until introduced to the work of Antoni Gaudí and Erich Mendelsohn. Goff noticed Prince's work on a lecture tour, and asked the young student to work for him. Prince worked for Goff in 1970–71, and continued to collaborate with his ex-boss after setting up on his own. When Goff died in 1982, Prince inherited a commission for a Japanese art gallery in Los Angeles to house the Price Collection.

It is rare for a client to be as closely linked to architectural culture as his architect. But Joe Price could point to links with organicism stretching back three generations, much further than Prince. Price had pushed his oil-magnate father to commission Frank Lloyd Wright for one of the architect's only two high rises, the Price tower (1956) in Oklahoma, and then got assigned by his father to work on the project. Then Price visited Japan, meeting his future wife Etsuko and starting his famous collection of Japanese art. On his

return, Price commissioned Goff in 1956 to design him a house in Bartlesville, Oklahoma. That commission took until 1976 to complete, when Goff turned his attention to the art gallery.

On Goff's death, Prince was a natural replacement. His own work had shown links to organic architecture while pointing to a baroque approach of his own. The O'Brien residence, White Rock, New Mexico (1974–75), was his first commission on being qualified. The house played circles off squares and triangles, but the geometry was converted into a somewhat disappointingly angular elevation. A more successful exploitation of such wild floor plans is seen in Prince's own house, in Albuquerque, New Mexico (1983–84). Here, a tubular volume is raised above the view of neighbours on four structural and service cores, each pair surrounded by two larger cylinders of rooms. Polychromatic tiles, tongue-and-groove decking, sun canopies, and black structural steel all add up to an appropriate richness; its shiplike appearance recalls Wright's Marin County Civic Centre (1957–66).

The Price house, like Prince's own house, seeks privacy: it is a plot squeezed between others. But where Prince overlooks neighbours, the Price family also has the sea. The plan turns two ways, building up a windowless zone of rooms against adjoining properties, but opening out towards the views of the Pacific Ocean. The house, therefore,

The heart of the house is a quiet pool, crossed by a simple bridge. Bedrooms for the family lie on either side. Prince's vocabulary of wood, matched by his expressive structure in which apparent tree trunks hold up each pod, transforms an architectural space in something which approaches the organic architecture so enjoyed by Gaudí and even Wright – the creation of an almost mystical environment, like a folkloric stage set.

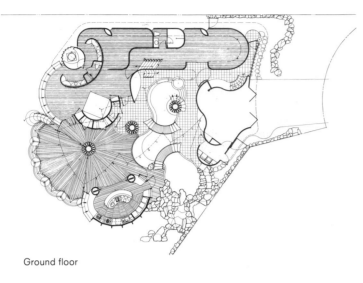

Ground floor

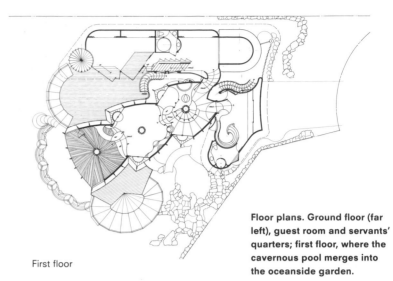

First floor

Floor plans. Ground floor (far left), guest room and servants' quarters; first floor, where the cavernous pool merges into the oceanside garden.

offers the street a mound of overlapping shingles punctured by a single door. Strangely, the door opens on to Joe Price's study, the rest of the house reached from behind his desk.

The formal core of the house rests in three pods, gradually stepping down towards the sea view. Each one is supported by a trunk of fir, its branches forming the ceiling and walls of each room. The gaps are then filled with an extraordinary richness of materials such as teak and stained glass, and sometimes left open to frame the sea view from the deck of the lowest level. The rest of the house is reached down a flight of stairs, which descends through the living core of the house to the swimming pool, which is crossed by bridges, and entrances to family rooms.

The house fits its label. Organic architecture does not seek to divide and rule – all parts of a building flow naturally into one another. The Price house obscures the distinction between roof and walls, both externally with the shingle or copper cladding, and internally with the glue-laminated wooden structure. Pods flow seamlessly into one another. And the organic interior, so often a cocoon of confused spaces, is given precise definition by Prince's cavernous arrangement around the pool.

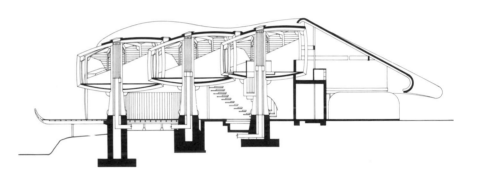

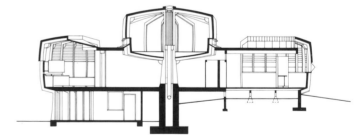

Long section (above) from the ocean through three pods to the street entrance. Cross-section (right) with the more traditional rooms on either side of the elevated pod.

The whole house focuses on a balcony (right) from which the family can enjoy spectacular views of the Pacific Ocean. Even this 'outdoor' element is protected by its overhang of shingles.

Like his hero Bruce Goff, Prince either does not use typical materials or uses typical materials in an unusual way. Thus the interior (left) is a mixture of man-made fabrics, wood and stained glass. Steps descend to the cavernous core (above).

Mario Botta
Casa Bianda

Losone, Ticino, Switzerland, 1987–89

Mario Botta, unlike other members of the Ticinese Tendenza such as Luigi Snozzi does not stick to pure Corbusian forms. Instead he shapes his path towards organic architecture by picking, choosing and gathering from several other post-war models.

Kenneth Frampton, the US-based critic, has identified six recurring features of Mario Botta's work, five of which appear in the Casa Bianda. The house is a marker; its principal staircase is in a structural module; cutaways focus on distant views; the interior is largely open plan; and a recessed atrium indicates living rooms on the *piano nobile*. That Botta's work can be defined by such distinct elements suggests an architectural genealogy of condensed diversity.

If Luigi Snozzi represents the original neo-Corbusian inclinations of the Ticinese Tendenza, then Botta offers another, later approach by this Swiss school of serious modern architects. Snozzi's houses are formed by the primacy of the function and built to machine aesthetics (see Casa Bernasconi, page 47). Botta's domestic work is equally rational, but displays the skilful amalgamation of a far wider range of great modern architects.

Perhaps the difference between the two is one of generations. Snozzi matured as an architect during the heroic period of modernism. Botta came of age when those former certainties were being questioned. His apprenticeship in the late 1950s, for example, was with Tita Carloni, one of the early post-war Ticinese architects who turned to the organicism of Frank Lloyd Wright to escape the era's scorn for context or scale – what the Italian architectural critic Francesco dal Co calls the

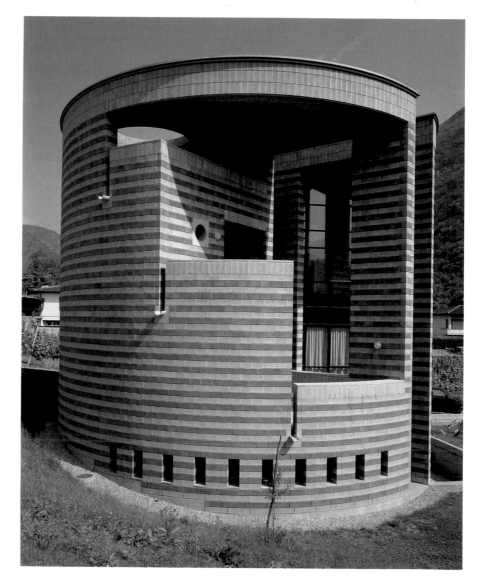

The Casa Bianda is the product of a learning curve which includes the Casa Rotonda Stabio (1981), with its circular floorplan (left), and the Villa at Cadenazzo, Ticino (1971), with its Kahnian circles (below).

Inside the Casa Bianda, Botta's cutaways and piers provide the family with a variety of voluminous rooms which are still protected from prying eyes.

'schematic reductions achieved by radical Swiss architecture'.

The lessons of observation and assimilation were not lost on Botta. He spent much of the 1960s at university in Venice, surrounded by an unbelievably rich group of teachers. His professor, Giuseppe Mazzariol, played a key role in the city's commissioning of architects: Le Corbusier was asked to design Venice's new hospital and Louis Kahn the Palazzo dei Congressi. Botta got to work with both of them and then went on to have Carlo Scarpa as the tutor of his thesis. He experimented for a time with each master's ideas before developing an architectural identity of his own.

The Stabio house (1966-67), for example, is an unashamed assemblage of Corbusian elements, with its *in situ* concrete staircase standing apart from the house, its strip of horizontal windows, and its upper storey raised on *pilotis*. But four years later, the Cadenazzo house (1971) displays an altogether different set of priorities with its box-like exterior of exposed masonry punctured by huge, Kahnian circles. Such geometry was not merely decorative but a device used by Botta to enunciate semi-private, semi-public loggias around the entrances to the house. The Riva San Vitale house (1973) develops this theme to its limit, leaving the structure of the house in isolation behind a three-storey portico.

Botta's references to other architects suggest a

The house at Riva San Vitale, Ticino (1973), provides a model for the Casa Bianda's deep voids and entrance bridge.

selective harvest rather than wholesale plagiarism. He does not stick dogmatically to Le Corbusier's 'five points' of the 1920s, like Tadao Ando (see the Kidosaki house, page 65), preferring, instead, to enjoy only Le Corbusier's principles of light, orientation and climate. And how much of the Kahnian vocabulary overlaps with the Scarpa-inspired interest in tectonics and the vernacular? Francesco dal Co argues for the influence of Kahn; Kenneth Frampton cites four specifically Ticinese types of buildings – bird-catching towers, four-pier agrarian shelters, two-tone local brickwork; and traditional drying barns. Wherever the balance lies, Botta had one more dose to come.

Robert Venturi's seminal Mother's house (1960-62) and SITE's BEST supermarket (intermediate façade showroom), Houston (1974), were some of the final blows to dogmatic modernism, providing intellectual justification and acceptable instructions for such former architectural taboos as decoration and figurativeness. Botta did not look to either as post-modern apologists: a central cleft or cut, not dissimilar from devices used by Venturi or SITE, organizes both plan and façade while revealing and/or obscuring the house behind.

Now Botta has evolved the final ordering of his own architecture, producing a stream of houses from the 1970s that can finally be called his own.

The Casa Bianda belongs effortlessly to this mature phase of his work. The four-storey house is

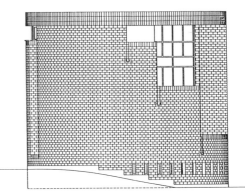

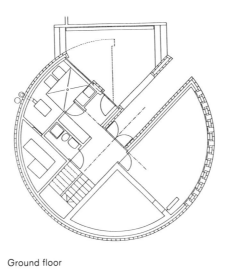

Floor plans: ground floor, entrance, stores and guests; first floor, family bedrooms; second floor, living room; roof.

Ground floor

Second floor

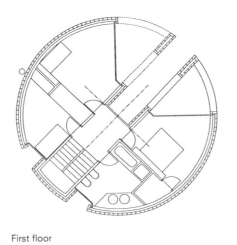

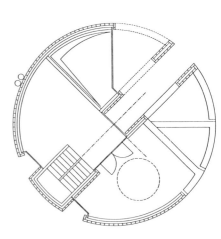

First floor

Roof

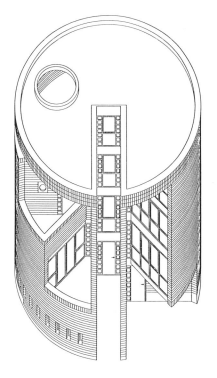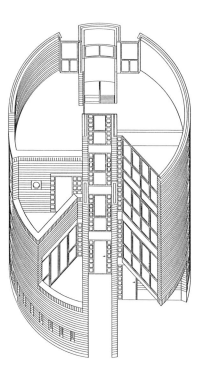

The split in the façade sets up an axis through the plan of the house, defining the entrance and circulation. But a more important feature is Botta's complex geometry for each plan, which divides the house up in section like a cake from which slices have been cut.

situated in the dip of a beautiful Ticinese valley, surrounded by the dull domestic products of the prosperous Swiss bourgeois. Botta does not position his building to relate to either neighbours or the immediate vicinity. Instead, the house is oriented to the beauty of the garden and the distant hills. But Botta's houses have never hugged the sloping Ticinese terrain, being objects rather than subjects in the landscape. And this house, at a level far lower than the adjacent street, is reached by a bridge to an alternative entrance that leads directly into the second floor.

A circular floor plan confirms the exclusivity. The Casa Bianda, like a cake with a few slices cut out, rises as a tower of double-banded brickwork. The accommodation is arranged with entrance and stores at ground level, bedrooms at first floor and living room at second. The order places priority on the views and sorts out the entrances. The real front door, which is not the entrance reached across the bridge, lies at the centre of the circle, approached through the characteristic axial cleft, this time, between two brick piers.

One of the piers stands in isolation, framing one side of a cutaway that rises through the full height of the house. The other pier also frames a cutaway, but one that emerges more slowly as the wall steps back in three balconies, each one separated by characteristic dripstones. The play of voids in both plan and elevation created a façade that is both intimate and revealing; the piers obscure the house behind but the voids allow the heart of the house to be observed from outside. The vocabulary emphasizes the distinction between Casa Bianda and its neighbours, defining Botta's house as a marker within the landscape.

Xaveer de Geyter
House in Brasschaat

Antwerp, Belgium, 1990–93

Some of the key elements in the design of the Brasschaat house provide a clue to the origins of its architect. Xaveer de Geyter was the project architect on the Villa dall'Ava in Paris, designed by Rem Koolhaas' OMA (see page 100). Therefore, he, like Koolhaas and many of de Geyter's contemporaries in the Flemish-speaking areas of the Low Countries, has broken with the area's modernist past to develop an architecture that explores the aesthetics of construction.

The influence on the Brasschaat house is most immediately apparent in the garden/rear elevation. Here, the one-storey house is resolved in a sliding glass wall where each pane/door is held within a heavy steel frame over which a flat roof floats. The composition is one close to the pavilion-like ideals of Mies van der Rohe, where the creation of a purely rational façade makes no reference to context. Koolhaas' earlier villa at Kralingen or the Kunsthal in Rotterdam (see page 104) both have at least one similar elevation, though each building is intimately locked into its location.

De Geyter belongs to a younger generation than Koolhaas, though one that follows its master's radical break with the Dutch past and finds location a challenge rather than an inconvenience. This part of Flanders is most suitable. Brasschaat has all the trappings of extreme wealth: manicured kerbsides, vulgar houses, and children driven to school in Mercedes. Yet, this American-style suburb

Although Xaveer de Geyter's Brasschaat house looks like a Miesian pavilion from the outside, the garden façade gives little indication of the status of the house within.

Rooms are arranged in zones, with a conservatory nearest the garden and one on either side of the internal courtyard.

De Geyter inverts the normal domestic routine by placing the garage and the entrance above the house. This policy is explained by the presence of a sand dune, an original feature of the site, which has been left in place to shield the house from the street.

sits on Kalmthout heath, a vast expanse of sand dunes and pine forest, and smells and feels like the Hamptons or Les Landes though stranded inland. Most houses utterly ignore this context, with inconvenient hillocks levelled for foundations and natural vegetation replaced by horticulture.

Two sisters were given adjoining parcels of Brasschaat land by their father. They then chose two of Belgium's best young talents as their architects. One sister picked Stéphane Beel for her almost-level, rectangular plot dominated by mature oaks. Beel accommodated such spectacular nature by designing one of his more usual white villas (see page 82) – a two-storey house, its perimeter a series of small garden courts, its view of the trees framed by *brise-soleils*. The other sister chose de Geyter for her quite different adjacent plot, which was separated from the street by a pine-covered dune. Client and architect had no desire to remove the obstacle, seeing it as a rich starting-point for the design.

The one-storey house is located directly behind the dune, little of it visible from the street except for the garage and entrance – two geometric shapes, a square and a triangle, rising from the ridge of the dune. A drive leads to the crest, cruising through the pines. Here, the car is parked in the garage, which has walls of thin, vertically arranged, oblong glass blocks. A ramp covered by the sloping form of the corrugated, metal-clad

triangle then leads down to the house. The villa is arranged in a series of parallel strips, starting at the garden side and running back into the dune. The order creates rooms, ranked by their various degrees (as in geometry) of views – out or up. The first strip, for example, is the living room and study, which is separated from the garden by the glass wall. The rooms act almost like a conservatory to the interior of the house.

The second layer includes a dining room and the main bedroom on either side of the first internal courtyard. Views are still possible through to the garden beyond and into the courtyard. A service/circulation core then runs through the heart of the house, dissected by the ramp down from the roof and partitioned to provide bathrooms, kitchen and stores. The apartment for the children runs along the back of the house, parallel to a retaining wall cut into the dune. Rooms here do not have views to the garden, but look out into two smaller internal courtyards or up to the top of the dune. The trunks of the pine trees are 2 metres (6 feet, 6 inches) above ground level at this point, their permanent dark foliage a contrast to the sky above.

De Geyter creates an order of colour and character running through the house. The patios, for example, are different: that of the living room is paved and cleverly plays off the indoor fireplace; one of the two at the rear hints at the serenity of a

Ground floor

Roof

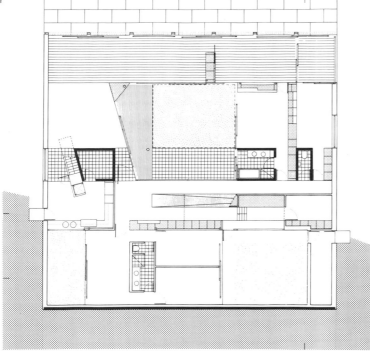

Japanese garden, the other is to be enjoyed in the morning. And while the exterior of the house is colourless, the interior has different materials for each part: light blue-greenish tiles towards the garden; wooden floors in the living room; profiled aluminium cladding for the main staircase. Wooden bookshelves and cupboards are used to divide up the space.

The client and her husband agreed with each other on some of the programme for the house. Both wanted studies, direct access to the garden at the rear and a semi-self-contained weekend apartment for their university-aged children. But the client wanted a modest street presence, her husband something a little more theatrical. Ironically, de Geyter met the demands of one with those of the other, for the house, despite its apparent modesty, could not make a stronger impression on its surroundings. Most neighbours in Brasschaat show off their mock-Tudor or faux-Georgian façades. De Geyter, instead, inverts bourgeois sensibilities, displaying the elements most houses choose to hide, such as the garage, and spotlighting the result at night.

Ground floor and roof plans. The lower level is quite clearly divided into a rational zoning of strips, broken by three internal courtyards while the upper level is arranged like large pieces of garden furniture.

Garden and west elevations. The typical Miesian pavilion becomes a late twentieth-century model of the house at one with its landscape.

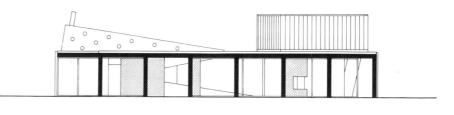

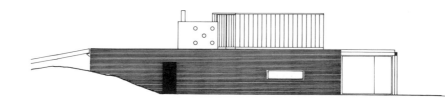

Nonda Katsalidis

St Andrews house

Mornington Peninsula, Victoria, Australia, 1991

Over the last ten years the beach house has become something of an icon for Australian architects. One reason for this interest lies in the challenge of developing a sensibility which is more appropriate to the wild than to the more usual environment of the city or suburb.

Harry Seidler, the Austrian-born Australian, introduced the international style to Australian domestic architecture with a series of houses in Sydney between 1949 and 1954, characterized by a Miesian parti. The injection of such ideas from the northern hemisphere, like so much of recent Australian architectural history, is a story of gradual assimilation until the form has acquired a national characteristic all of its own.

Glenn Murcutt's houses have, for example, explored an architecture suitable for the Australian environment (see page 225). Yet the characteristic barrel-vaulted or butterfly roof forms and louvred glazed walls still rise from the basic Miesian floor plan. The layout of Nonda Katsalidis' St Andrews house follows similiar rules, with the living room lying beyond an enfilade of bedrooms and bathrooms. He, however, like Murcutt, develops the plan until a house, constructed on an entirely rational basis of manufactured products, becomes part of its context; a 'pavilion that is both part of and yet stands apart from the landscape'.

That the St Andrews house is placed more in than on its surroundings is made explicit by Katsalidis' inspirations and interpretations. For this Melbourne-based architect, the house represents his first new-build domestic project. Other work has included extensions to existing Victorian and Edwardian houses, such as the King Residence in Hampton (1988) and the Deutscher

Although the St Andrews house is unashamedly aware of some of the principles of international style, such as the Miesian parti, Katsalidis has undoubtedly broken away from its dogma. For this is a house (above) which acknowledges such vital factors as views, context and the sun's orientation.

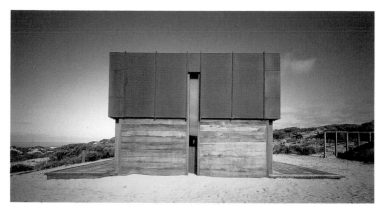

The house also picks up on part of the Australian myth. The walls, for example, which are made from recycled timber, give the impression of a house which has been assembled from packing crates washed up on the shore. This image has particular resonance in a country where most of the inhabitants or their ancestors arrived by sea.

Corten steel clads the upper half of the living room. The material turns the lower-level windows into a framing device for the surrounding views of the sea and the dunes.

Nonda Katsalidis' extension to the King Residence in Hampton (1988).

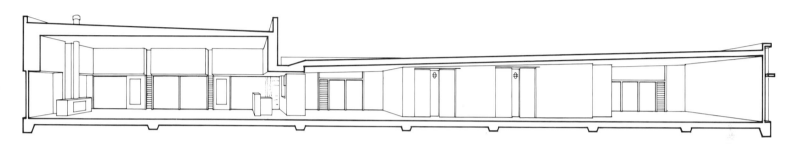

Gallery and home (1988). His biggest commissions are products of the commercial office boom of the 1980s – two office towers in downtown Melbourne.

So, the St Andrews house represents something of a departure; a building type without precedence in Katsalidis' workload and outside his more habitual urban or suburban locations. For the St Andrews house sits on a sand dune facing the ocean, a location more similar to the windswept scrub of Barrie Marshall's Phillip Island (see page 120) than the more temperate coast further north of Daryl Jackson's house at Bermagui (see page 86). Such difficult conditions inspired an 'exploration of the early Australian buildings that were cut from virgin forests and erected as defences against an alien land'.

Katsalidis also turned to some of the first building types unique to Australia, which were developed to meet its growing economy. He cites examples such as the 'wool stores, wineries, wharfs, rock crushers and the Queensland houses that unashamedly displayed their stud wall construction to the ouside world'. They were rich, though varied, models, somewhat at odds with the strict dogma of modern architecture. Just as Murcutt translated the organicism of a bark shelter into a man-made abstraction, so Katsalidis saw that 'the challenge was to fuse these sentimental vernacular sources with the formal traditions at the core of modernism'. The elevations, therefore,

The house is on one level throughout, although Katsalidis has not avoided manipulating volumes. The living room, for example, is an enjoyable double-height space, while the bedrooms are a more functional one storey.

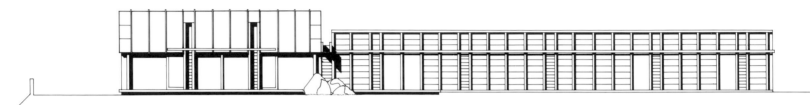

A rainwater gulley emphasizes the transition between bedrooms and living room, wood and steel, double height and single storey. Its role, besides utility, is emphasized by the small pile of big rocks onto which the rain splashes.

come in two halves. The living room is a double-height space, its top half clad in corten steel, its bottom half filled on two sides with glass. A rainwater gulley, open at either end to allow rainwater to drip on to rocks arranged on the ground below, separates the living room from the bedrooms. The division, though obvious, is rather unnecessary considering the nature of the bedroom block. There, walls are covered in recycled timber, as if the sea had washed up a packing case, once the container of a settler's possessions transported to a new world. The clarity of the association with Australia's immigrant origins merely reinforces Katsalidis' success, welding figuratism to modernism, rationalism to landscape.

One key to that link is Katsalidis' interest in finding a way for the St Andrews house to 'develop a dialogue with its surroundings'. He continues, 'colour helps make the connections that a building seeks to have with its site. The influence of the elements on the materials modifies colour, and the special qualities of the local light bring out their uniqueness.' So the wood elevations of the bedroom block, left untreated, can look like that washed-up crate; the corten steel above the living room windows can pick up on the russet tones of the surrounding vegetation and can glow in the setting sun.

Such intercourse between climate and building relies on Katsalidis' site planning. The house sits on the ridge of the dune, running along an east–west

The floor plan (left) is a
response to location. The
bedrooms, for example, are
kept to that side of the
building which has the best
views of the sea. Circulation,
meanwhile, is kept to the
north side of the building
where views are unnecessary
but protection from the
summer sun is welcome.

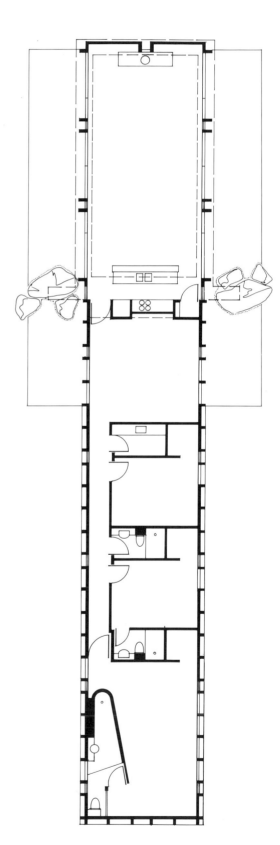

axis to minimize exposure to the winds. River
pebbles over the roof help to insulate and stabilize
the bitumen roof. The orientation also maximizes
exposure to the winter sun from the north and to
the ocean views from the south. Katsalidis takes
advantage of this opportunity with the living room
windows, which are totally double-glazed,
exploiting the potential for light and distractions.

Yet, the architect has chosen to limit the
exposure of the exterior by bringing the opaque
corten steel cladding halfway down the elevation.
This device turns a window into a frame,
converting a landscape into a picture. That, with its
classical connotations, returns Katsalidis firmly
back to the rational realm of Mies van der Rohe.

Scogin Elam & Bray
Chmar house

Atlanta, Georgia, USA, 1989

No house, apart from Lloyd Wright's Fallingwater, could fit more perfectly into its landscape. Even the bedroom balcony of the Chmar house rests among the trees.

The buildings of Scogin Elam & Bray can be interpreted as having been inspired by the two sides of Frank Lloyd Wright's organic legacy: his interest in locating buildings in the perfect spot, such as at Fallingwater; and the later period of Wright's work where the helicoid plan takes precedence: think here of the David Wright house (1950) in Phoenix, or the Guggenheim Museum in New York (1959).

The Chmar house appears, at first, to fulfil both criteria. Its location in its woodland site, for example – a clearing created by a fallen tree – is chosen with a similar care to that of Fallingwater. SEB's means of expressing such empathy, however – for the Chmar house is full of the angular geometries and cantilevers more common to deconstruction, a style more usually seen in the city – seems to be radically at odds with the tranquillity of a virgin forest. How can such an apparent contradiction be resolved?

Atlanta-based SEB often deals with the world of the American suburb, the retail strips where empty building sites are squeezed between the multi-media icons of drive-thru America. Here, the practice has tried to achieve an architecture it terms popular yet remarkable among the contextless wastes; the result is an architecture successfully alien to its surroundings. Buckhead library (1989), in an up-and-coming suburb of Atlanta, for example, is definitely

Despite Scogin Elam & Bray's constant respect for context, they also know how to control it. Thus, while the Chmar house is everything the client wanted and fits within its location, it also plays a part in a far wider architectural debate: is it deconstruction or merely a sensible rearrangement of rooms in a time-honoured modernist tradition?

The decks (opposite) and the stairs (right) help to forge links between this human insertion into the landscape and the wood itself. Even the telegraph poles rising through the decks act as a reminder of the sometimes ironic similarity between technology and nature.

deconstructionist. Morrow library (1991), in a more family-oriented suburb, has its terracotta-coloured walls decorated with the prints of local children's hands.

The Chmar house, though, is for a private client and, in addition, is in a very different type of location. The clues to its appearance lie not just with the libraries but also in two houses by SEB (two incomplete projects). The Weekend house and the Roderique house are both in beautiful settings, but one is for a busy city couple, the other for a large family with children, nanny, occasional grandparents and frequent guests. Just as the libraries display some of the characteristics of their end-users, so these two houses reveal the diversity of the two clients.

The Weekend house, for example, is the guest house for a larger house to be built some time in the future on the site of an old overgrown estate. The very casualness of weekends and the variety of future guests are some of the defining characteristics for the house. A series of sliding walls/doors subdivides the house for multiple uses and frees up the plan. The device is carried through to the elevations, where other walls/doors can be pulled back to break down divisions between inside and out and even alter its appearance – voids become solid blocks and vice versa.

The Roderique house has a far more complicated and introverted plan, created by the characters of

Scogin Elam & Bray's deconstructivist tendencies are shown (top) in the Buckhead library, Atlanta (1989) and the more Chmar-like qualities of the unbuilt Weekend house (above).

many individuals and their activities. The formal dining and living room are some way off on their own, placed neatly beside a lawn. Yet, the kitchen, toy store, family dining and living room are a pickle of intertwining and overlapping geometries. Upstairs, the use of curves to emphasize the youthful exuberance of the children's bedrooms contrasts with the straight lines of the parents' bedrooms, which stress the sedateness of maturity. The resulting elevations are a mass of shapes and cantilevers.

The Chmar family is different yet again, as they belong to an obscure Japanese religious sect. Their beliefs look for daily inspiration from light before an ancestral altar in a Goshinden room at the heart of a house. In more practical terms, the Chmars were seeking a house that was at one with its precious surroundings, and that provided all the bedrooms, kitchen and living rooms for an average family without destroying its surroundings.

SEB raised the main two-storey part of the house on concrete foundations as the site sloped away to the north. Another semi-detached one-storey guest wing is similarly raised, allowing a car port to be hidden below. The elevation of the two blocks leaves the forest floor largely untouched. The two parts of the house run perpendicular to each other, producing a plan that Scogin compares to a pen knife with its bottle opener and shallow blade extended. This is how his imagery works: one deck

The living room of the Chmar house (right) picks up on the woodlike exterior and benefits from the full width of the building's footprint.

The façade (top and above), which looks like a multi-faceted screen, ensures a superior quality of light is shed into the interior.

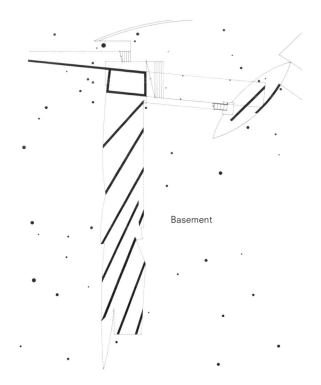

Basement

Site plan. The house lies away from a suburban main road but its exact location was dictated by a clearing in the woods created by a fallen tree.

is cantilevered razor sharp over the slope and into the woods; the other deck is more traditional but for the five telegraph poles that rise up through it. The length and breadth of the decks break down the division as to where the house stops and the wood begins.

Such architectural reticence was evidently a requirement of the brief, but one SEB takes to its limit. The grey, concrete-like render of the exterior reduces much of the façade to a mere backdrop for winter shadows or summer foliage. Yet, the potential monotony of such a finish is relieved by the windows. The redwood frames stand in marked contrast to their grey surrounds, and their various shapes, from simple oblongs through to horizontal panels, create a dramatic syncopation of forms. The variety of windows is not mere whimsy. Each one relates logically to its context. Strongly horizontal windows, for example, rise double-height through the thickest part of the main wing, illuminating the ground-floor living room and the Goshinden room elevated at first floor above.

The redwood also sets the tone for the interior. The floors are covered in sheets of composite chipboard, their randomness imitating the fallen leaves outside. And the two staircases are studies in carpentry; one a traditional set of steps and risers in birch and redwood up to the Goshinden room, the other a composition of plywood panels up to the children's bedrooms.

The forms of the Chmar house and the two others by SEB beg the question whether a house can fit into the landscape despite espousing a style more often associated with the city; between the Wrightian context and the city-slickness of deconstruction. Yet, there is another explanation. Deconstruction can be interpreted not simply as some stand-alone development but as a natural and inevitable progression by the post-war European avant-garde, such as Rem Koolhaas' OMA (see page 100). This theory argues that deconstruction takes the Miesian parallel arrangement of rooms – the German pavilion in Barcelona (1929), for example – and uses it not in plan but in section. And what inspired Mies but a similar order of rooms in Wright's Prairie houses?

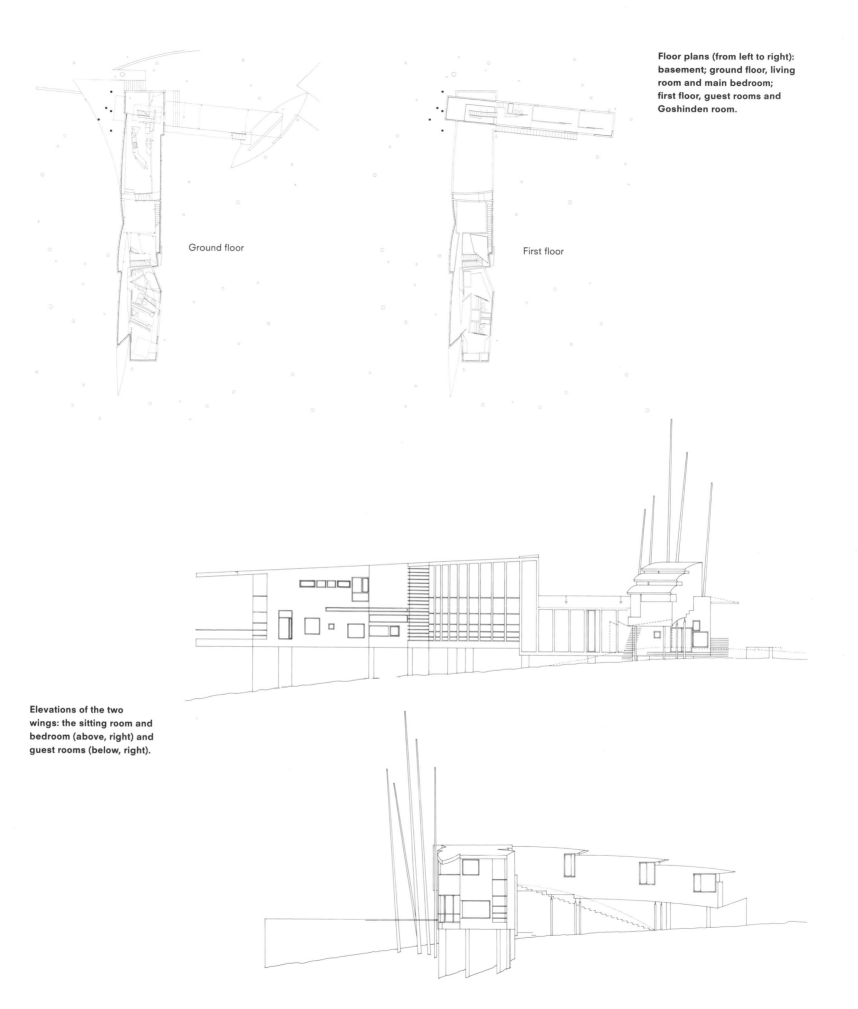

Floor plans (from left to right): basement; ground floor, living room and main bedroom; first floor, guest rooms and Goshinden room.

Ground floor

First floor

Elevations of the two wings: the sitting room and bedroom (above, right) and guest rooms (below, right).

Enric Miralles
Casa Garau-Agusti

Belaterra, Barcelona, Spain, 1988–93

Barcelona's architects, released from the Franco regime, liberated by the rejuvenation of Catalan culture and made prominent by the run-up to the 1992 Olympics, have spent the past ten years reconnecting with the region's architectural culture.

Enric Miralles, a Barcelona-based architect, sits comfortably within these developments. His most notable works to date include a cemetery outside Barcelona (1987-91), where concrete beams and retaining walls create a valley to the dead; the archery range for the 1992 Barcelona Olympics, in which most of the facilities are covered in dramatic, cantilevered roofs; and now the Casa Garau-Agusti, another poetic exploration of geometries and plans. The resulting forms have all too easily been interpreted as deconstructivist, not unlike the work of Scogin Elam and Bray (see page 176), their exuberance an advertisement to every avant-garde, European, architectural groupie. But Miralles' work, like that of SEB, rests on stable ground, belonging, instead, firmly within the cultural and historical framework of his Catalonian homeland.

The social, economic and, not least, architectural history of the area has encouraged Catalan architects to avoid the lack of context and universal character of much post-war, international modernism, developing, instead, an identifiably regional, post-war modernism. A comparison can be made with the Ticino, the Italian-speaking region of Switzerland, where the region's relative isolation

The stepped entrance façade (left) of the house provides privacy within the confines of a narrow, off-street suburban site. The bedroom (right) at the end of the house is left as a viewing-point over the nearby valley.

has ensured the survival, and now development, of a strand of early modernism, as seen in the work of Luigi Snozzi (see page 44) and Mario Botta (see page 156). Catalonia, like the Ticino, boasts its own minority language, but the reaction to the lifting of the political suppression of the Franco era turned regional pride into raw nationalism.

That conflict has turned post-Franco Spain into a country of two architectures: one, the purist, contextless buildings of architects such as Madrid-based Alberto Campo Baeza (see page 56); the other, an architecture where provincial cities can boast a strong, independent identity (Seville's Cruz and Ortiz, and Barcelona's Miralles and Torres and Lapeña). One reason for Barcelona's individuality is the juxtaposition of its urban grid and the surrounding mountains. The two meet in the suburbs, providing a particularly perverse type of building site for local architects. Antoni Gaudí faced the same sort of environment, his response being the Park Güell (1885-89) with its follies and pools exploiting the often peculiar geography; Miralles', more than a century later, is the Olympic archery range or cemetery.

The projects, by both Gaudí and Miralles, emphasize the existing features across the sites, such as river-beds, roads and fields, to develop a site plan determined intrinsically by context. Miralles' Casa Garau-Agusti is on a similarly awkward site, a strip-like plot running away and down from an

The crunched-up entrance (right) and back (below) elevations, dictated by the site, create spectacular volumes inside. One example is the shower room (above, right).

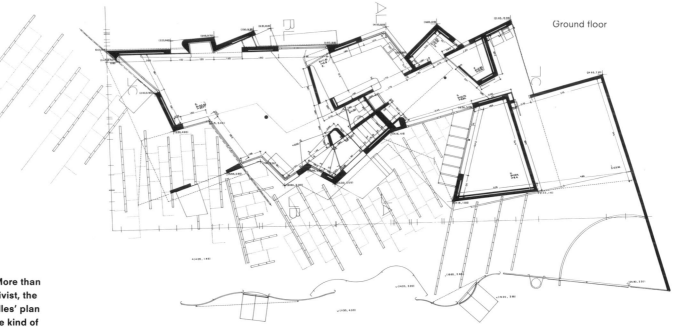

Ground floor

Site plan (below). More than simply deconstructivist, the geometries of Miralles' plan really pick up on the kind of architecture developed in the region during the 1950s by José Coderch.

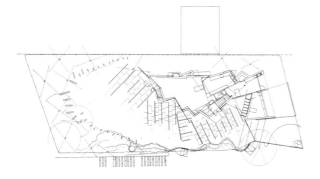

access road. Dull, suburban villas sit either side while a miraculous vision of a picturesque church lies across a shallow valley. Miralles places the house close to one side of the plot and very close to an adjacent house. The orientation opens up a breathing space on the entrance/main elevation of the house and leaves much of the garden free for views across to the church.

The footprint, or ground-floor plan, of the house is a product of this location. Its angularity, far from mere whimsy, is a condensation of existing view-lines, contours and avoidance of any visual contact with neighbouring buildings. The device also creates two very different elevations. There is the main elevation, its form broken by many large windows and its role in welcoming strangers or even the home-coming family emphasized by the heavy overhang of the roof. Then there is the rear elevation, only a metre or two from the property line. Miralles describes it as

the 'working façade' because of its chimney and kitchen door. But the various geometries create sight-lines out of the house and into a small, shady, strip garden of shingle and potted plants, but Miralles' method, refreshing though it seems, is far from new. A second, more important, reason for Barcelona's current regionalism stems from the work of José Coderch (1913-84), whose influence is unmistakable in the work of Torres and Lapeña, for example, in their house (1989) at Cap Martinet on Ibiza and no less so in the work of Miralles. Miralles sees Coderch as the missing member of Team X (the group of young architects, such as Aldo van Eyck, Giancarlo De Carlo, Peter and Alison Smithson, who, at the 10th international conference on modernism, CIAM X [1956], fought for a less rigid and rational modernism), interpreting the Spanish architect's manipulation of geometry as thinking about the space before starting, like the Smithsons.

Coderch's Casa Ugalda in Caldetes (1952) shows a similar sacrifice of floor plan to context as the Casa Garau-Agusti. Coderch's early sketches for the house show only where trees are located and views to the sea are possible. The resulting floor plan – a massive curved wall from which the rooms are built – has been described by David Mackay, the Barcelona-based architect, as cubes exploding into bent and curved forms to gather in the external views and immediate countryside.

The plan of the Casa Ugalda (1952) (top) by José Coderch is equally dictated by context, while Coderch's use of screens in the Barcelonata apartment block (1951) (above) occurs again in the Casa Garau-Agusti.

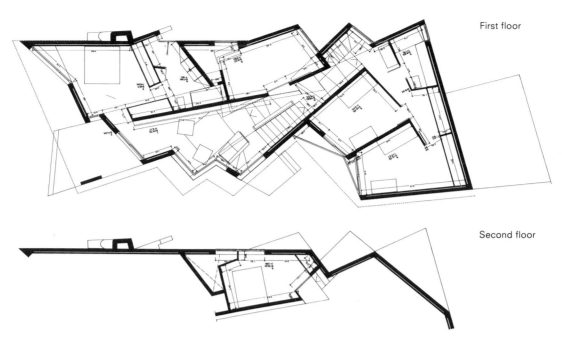

First floor

Second floor

Miralles' Casa Garau-Agusti follows other themes in Coderch's work. The green wooden shutters (contrasting with the orange-painted render over the wimple blocks of the walls) intended for the at-present partly naked I-beams above each window pay homage to Coderch's Barcelonata apartment block in Barcelona (1951), whose entire exterior elevation is a series of shutters. And the main elevation, a zigzag in plan, is intended to act just like a screen with furniture piled up one side, the garden furniture the other. The deliberate placement of furniture is a device used by Coderch in the Barcelonata apartments, where each flat's floor plan deliberately exploits what little space is available; beds either side of the entrance and the wardrobes on the building perimeter.

But Miralles' skill is to take the work of Coderch further. The Casa Garau-Agusti is the first domestic commission for Miralles. All his other projects have been within the public domain, making what some might see as a particularly élitist form of architecture rather more democratic. In the same way, Miralles saves the Casa Garau-Agusti from being just another architectural straitjacket/ statement by creating a series of spaces and rooms suitable for this family.

The juxtaposition of the sloping roof and geometry of the floor plans creates a variety of fascinatingly shaped rooms. The library at first floor, for example, has views of the church but also allows views down to the living room and across to the children's bedrooms. The adjacent study, apparently a closed room, has a mini-minstrel's gallery over the sitting room below. No room seems to follow simple bourgeois logic, forming, instead, overlapping rooms and circulation, corresponding to the complexity and relationships within a family.

This is, beyond doubt, a family home, where the L-shaped floor plan allows children in the bedroom to have clear views across to their parents, an arrangement quite similar to that in the house by Stéphane Beel (see page 83). And the core of the house is a small pottery used exclusively by Señora Agusti, placed so that she can clearly see arrivals to the house and any activity within the house, without leaving her wheel.

Eisaku Ushida/
Kathryn Findlay
Truss Wall house

Tsurukawa, Machida-City, Japan, 1991–93

The Japanese suburb, with its typical detached
family house squashed on to a plot more suitable
for something smaller, has little of the grace of its
American or Australian equivalent. Young
architects have developed a domestic architecture
that turns houses into introverted blocks, where
a courtyard creates an idealized alternative to
the exterior.

Ushida/Findlay houses, such as their earlier
Echo Chamber house (1989) and the later Truss
Wall house (1991–93), create their own
environment – one that is enclosed by a wall and
centred around a courtyard. This technique has
its foundations in the work of Tadao Ando (see
page 70). Ushida/Findlay's work, however, goes way
beyond the narrow confines of Ando's Corbusian
language to create a Japanese house type of their
own with roots very distant from Ando's.

The individuality of their work reflects a search
for identity: 'Japanese houses, in the past 30 years,
have become like everything else – cars, washing
machines – conceived around mass production,
with the only differences between them being the
expensive add-ons the owner can select, like fancy
toilets, security systems and rice cookers.'
Ushida/Findlay believe, instead, that the 'home is
the basis for your life and it should be a very
special place'.

So, their houses are organized like a journey
through a mini-landscape, where a courtyard

The living room on the first
floor opens directly into an
intensely private courtyard.
The pink 'pavers' are
achieved by using balloons
filled with wet concrete
which, when dry, creates
these sensual shapes.

The method of construction – using wire mesh pumped full of concrete – allows Ushida/Findlay to develop an architecture which expresses an organic curvaceousness both in plan and section.

For the earlier Echo Chamber house (1989), Ushida/Findlay only managed to achieve such fluidity in plan, although the berm wall that surrounds the site hints at the later Truss Wall house.

offers an abridgement of the countryside and the activities of the family a précis of everyday life. The buildings become paradigms of Japan's chaotic cities but are protected from the noise and squalor of their surroundings. Much the same could be said of Ando's work, but Ushida/Findlay seek a more spiritual response from their clients, leaving them to 'explore the subtle and unending layers of meaning in the typology, triggering associations and memories in their subconscious', as the architects say.

Frank Gehry makes much the same sort of comments about his own domestic architecture (see page 132), saying, 'images can relate to all kinds of symbolic things; ideas you have liked, places you have liked, bits and pieces of your life that you would like to recall'. Gehry's geometric shapes, however, appear firmly literal compared with Ushida/Findlay's lucid abstract forms that link them firmly to organic architecture. The architects, though, are keen to distance themselves from that definition, saying that the word 'organic' suggests an architecture that 'already exists which is clumsy and heavy'. They see their work as far from that; one that creates, instead, a very precise and economic architecture expressed in 3-D spaces. The Truss Wall house crystallizes that difference, which has evolved from the earlier Echo Chamber.

The site of the Echo Chamber, located on a quiet tree-lined suburban street, is enclosed in a light-

Most of the furniture inside (right) is fitted – traditional furniture, after all, would scarcely be appropriate – allowing the architects to express their adventurousness in materials and shapes yet further. Indeed much of the house, beside the furniture, also feels 'fitted' – the stairs to the rooftop patio (below) both providing access and imparting yet more action to the house's lively imagery.

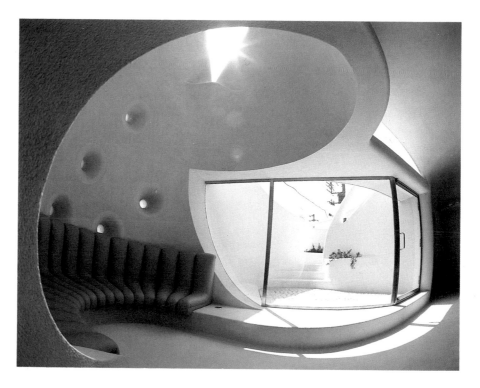

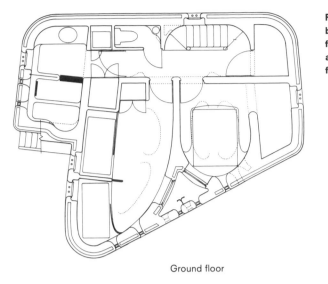

Floor plans: ground floor, bedrooms and bathrooms (left); first floor, living/dining room and kitchen (right); second floor, rooftop patio (far right).

Ground floor

ochre berm wall which rises to eye-level. The house, in section, is firmly within the tradition of contemporary modern Japanese houses, with its courtyard and box-like bedrooms suspended on steel beams at an upper storey. Where Ushida/Findlay depart from their peers is in plan. People enter from the street and proceed through the ground-floor rooms, following an arc-shaped route which lets each room look on to another and ends in the womb-like curve of the bathroom. The circulation, together with the use of tiles and the small nooks in the berm wall, creates an interior rich in references to Bruce Goff.

The Truss Wall house goes further still, departing from the norm in both plan and section. The result is all the more commendable considering the ghastliness of the site, whose southern aspect unfortunately coincides with a view of the elevated main commuter line into Tokyo. Ushida/Findlay sought yet again to immunize the environment, though far more ingeniously than with the Echo Chamber. The house is on four levels, entered up a short flight of stairs to the upper living level. The sitting room is a double-height space, reaching into an alcove punctured with small, circular windows. The owners benefit from a view not of the trains roaring by, but of a small courtyard that, together with the stairs on to a grassed roof garden, takes up half the total floor space.

The porthole window onto the street is on the stairs leading from the entrance up to the first-level living room.

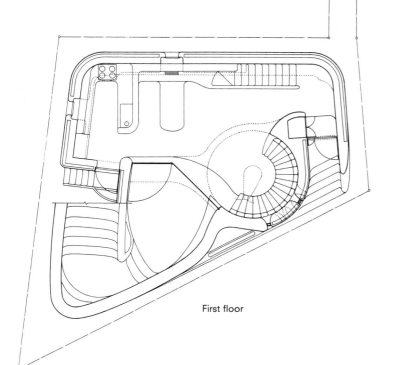

First floor

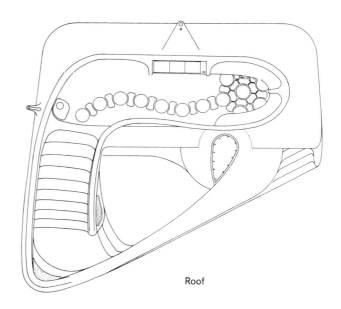

Roof

The children's and parents' bedrooms are one level below the living room, partially below street level. Light filters into the bedrooms through more portholes, though each room has a standard window set into an alcove, its privacy ensured by a low wall. Ushida/Findlay use this device to get light to the basement playroom through two windows further down the alcove. Much of the furniture is fitted to make the most efficient use of the available room, and the banquette is accompanied by a cantilevered dining table, long kitchen shelves and the parents' double beds. Each one picks up on the dynamic forms of the house made possible by the construction.

Indeed, what characterizes this house is the walls. The architects have developed a system where vertical trusses support wire mesh formed to any shape and then pumped full of concrete. This creates a double-skinned house, insulated from the heat in summer, the cold in winter and the noise of trains every day. The method also provides Ushida/Findlay with the most extraordinary flexibility, allowing the curvaceousness of the Echo Chamber plan to be carried through into the section of the Truss Wall house. The results are the powerful, sculptural forms of the house that take Ushida/Findlay, via the Echo Chamber house, from the work of Hans Scharoun (see page 110), through the traditions of Ando into an organic architectural language of their own.

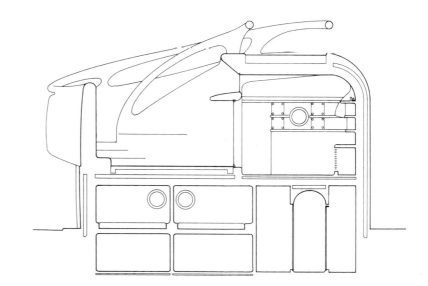

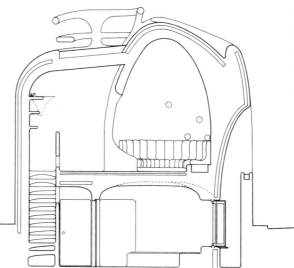

The long section (above) and cross section (left) through the house reveal just how much accommodation Ushida/ Findlay squeeze on to the restricted site.

Chapter 4

Urban compromise

Pierre Chareau, Maison de Verre, Paris, 1928-31.

The three previous chapters of this book indicate clearly the roots of three types of contemporary houses, charting their course from the early twentieth century. Each group follows a remarkably similar development pattern from the pre-twentieth-century model, through early twentieth-century classic, to late twentieth-century remake. But there is one type of modernist house that enjoys no such evolutionary clarity – the house in the city.

The ideal location for the modern movement house was always in the country rather than the city. The green field nature of such sites left the architect largely free to develop a design as fantastical as possible. Such freedom was a means of experimentation, each effort notching up one success or failure for the Modern Movement. But the city has been far more awkward, forcing the architect to confront the man-made inconveniences of neighbouring buildings, historic and largely unmovable street patterns, awkward and illogical planning authorities and fewer of the natural qualities, such as light and decent views, which are taken for granted in the country.

Take, for example, the houses by David Wild (see page 207) where the architect has been encouraged to accommodate the height set by the cornices of the adjacent Victorian houses, and to place windows to achieve the optimum view. Or, an even better example, perhaps, is Oakyard, by Allies

Le Corbusier, Maisons
La Roche and Jeanneret,
Paris, 1923-25.

and Morrison (see page 235) where the architects
are forced to use a pitched roof by the local
planning authorities despite the house's location
within a vast post-war housing estate of mainly
flat-roofed houses.

Yet, the situation has occasionally created
masterpieces, the urban compromise empowering
architects to find means to overcome the problems
and, in the process, creating memorable
masterpieces; think of Pierre Chareau's Maison
de Verre in Paris (1928–31), Le Corbusier's Maisons
La Roche and Jeanneret (1923–25), also in Paris, or
Le Corbusier's house for Dr Currutchet in La Plata
(1949). Each one provides later architects with
lessons on how to achieve the basic benefits of the
modern house: privacy, light and views.

The architecturally designed urban house, like
the country villa, began to reappear for the first
time since the end of the Roman era in sixteenth-
century Italy, where money, combined with
Renaissance aspirations, provided the impetus.
Palladio's villas, such as the Rotonda and Foscari
(page 23), drew on the traditions of these earlier
Roman villas, while his urban houses, such as the
Palazzo Thiene (1542) or the Palazzo Valmarana
(1565), drew on the traditions of ecclesiastical
palaces. The organization provided the form for
later urban houses.

The most important rooms were on the first
floor, creating a suitable sense of grandeur for

visitors but also obscuring the activities of the house from the prying eyes of the street. Shops and workshops filled the ground floor with activities suitable for the street. A central courtyard created every opportunity for providing natural light into the often deep plan of a typical city site and a small moment of peace within the constantly busy city. The organization sets the basic parameters of the urban house – industry on the ground floor, living on the first and sleeping above – a compromise between ideal living conditions and the reality of urban conditions.

New technology and novel aesthetics did little to change these basic rules with the Modern Movement house. Take Le Corbusier's La Roche and Jeanneret Houses (1923–25). The houses were commissioned by Le Corbusier's brother and the art collector La Roche, each one given their own, individual quarters by organizing the building in to two wings on an L-shaped floor plan. The main living rooms were placed on the first floor while the ground floor was left to accommodate the less aesthetic, though, in Le Corbusier's mind, equally worthy of a rational solution, parking and entry requirements.

The organization meets several criteria. The first-floor living rooms had vast windows, their elevated position ensuring privacy from nosy passers-by and a decent view, no different from a Renaissance palace. The logic of having the main living room on the first floor is followed by almost every architect in the next chapter. One example is Glenn Murcutt's house for Ken Done (see page 226) where the upper-storey living room enjoys both fantastic views of the nearby sea and privacy, despite the density of the local housing. The only exceptions to the rule are those houses, by Allies and Morrison (see page 235) or Hajime Yatsuka (see page 231), that are lucky enough to enjoy sufficiently spacious plots to have the main rooms on the ground floor.

The L-shaped plan provides another benefit. The Renaissance palace was often big enough to turn the central courtyard into something of a garden: think, here, of some of the later examples, such as the seventeenth-century *hôtels* of Paris' Marais district. Space is often too limited in the modern city for such luxuries but the Maisons La Roche and Jeanneret offer an alternative, not so much a courtyard as an outdoor space giving relative privacy.

Hajime Yatsuka does the same for his own house in Tokyo, conjuring a semi-courtyard out of Tokyo's nightmarish density in quite a different manner from either Tadao Ando (see page 70) or Ushida Findlay (see page 189). Such ambitions inform the house by Steve Christer and Margrét Hardardóttir (see page 217). The house they design is located in a suburb, but the division of the home into family house and guest quarters creates a house screened from the noise of traffic on an adjacent road. A courtyard, again far from fully enclosed, provides a welcome sanctuary.

What Le Corbusier's La Roche-Jeanneret model does not achieve, however, is a total exploitation of available light; there are big windows but there is little attempt to create a section within the house by which light can be drawn deep into the building – a basic benefit of the historic courtyard but now achieved by contemporary architects by use of an ingenious section. Perhaps the earliest example of this technique is the Maison de Verre by Pierre Chareau (1883–1950). The site for this house was an eighteenth-century *hôtel* in Paris, surrounded on all sides by apartment buildings. Architect and client, a Madame Dalsace, were intending to demolish the entire block and start afresh, but an elderly spinster on the second floor was a protected tenant. Chareau's solution was to demolish the ground and first floors, underpinning the second floor during reconstruction.

The space created became three floors in Chareau's design: the ground floor was the surgery for Madame Dalsace's husband, a gynaecologist; the first floor was the living room; and the new second floor the bedrooms and bathrooms. Such organization follows historical models, but Chareau showed how such traditions could be exploited using modern technology. The steel columns used in the underpinning became the final structure, allowing for a far greater manipulation of interior space than previous solid building techniques. Chareau, for example, took the goal of the central core even further at one point, creating a triple-height void from the entrance stairs up through the sitting rooms.

The Maison de Verre was left with a wonderful spaciousness and light in some of the most awkward of spaces. Contemporary architects have gone further, however, exploiting the potential of engineering to create something quite new. Frank Lloyd Wright's concept of the hearth had been developed from a house with one centre to the whole house being the centre; this principle is realized by Chareau and similarly informs the House with studio by Mecanoo (page 203). Studio and garage are on the ground floor, while living rooms, on the first, and bedrooms, on the second, surround a central void. The device allows the whole family to be constantly in touch with one another.

And, finally, there are views. Chareau rather muddies the water of the Maison de Verre with a façade of entirely opaque glass blocks; ideal for privacy but hopeless for contact with the outside world. Le Corbusier's house for Dr Currutchet finds an alternative method, turning, instead, to the ingenuity of section and plan. A garage and chauffeur's quarters were placed at street level with the surgery on the first, while living rooms, on the second, and bedrooms, on the third, lay above.

Le Corbusier, house for Dr Currutchet, La Plata, 1949.

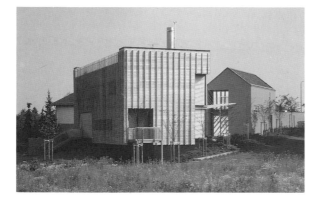

Studio Granda,
Haus im Vordentaunus,
Wiesbaden, 1989–92.

What makes the architecture work is Le Corbusier's organization of circulation using a ramp rising from street level, past the garage and to the door of the surgery and the house. The public (i.e. the patients) are therefore kept away from the house, which becomes something of a self-contained object two levels above the street. Le Corbusier took his design further, however, turning the roof of the surgery into a terrace for the living room above; the structural frame of the surgery extended upwards to form a *brise-soleil* for the terrace over the city below. The views out are deliberate, framed and controlled like those from Murcutt's Ken Done house or even David Wild's houses at Rochester Place.

Why, therefore, do urban houses enjoy less clarity in terms of architectural development? The answer must lie in the nature of contemporary architecture. Modern architecture has always been the art of the possible – anything goes – so that clients, architects and developers see architecture as little more than a catalogue of available styles.

Hajime Yatsuka, for example, clothes his house in Tokyo in two different styles; one a reference to Le Corbusier, the other to late nineteenth-century Austria. His reason: to give each part of the house an identity. Studio Granda breaks down the one-family house into two blocks, one in render, the other clad in wood; the practice's reasoning involves privacy, light and so on. Glenn Murcutt

rewrites his glass-and-steel style in the vocabulary of render for the Ken Done house: his reason – privacy.

The nature of contemporary architecture as a catalogue of styles is emphasized by the conditions of today's cities. Architecture used to seek solutions to problems such as urban density through a rationalization of the brief. Nowadays, architects prefer lazy references not merely to other architects' styles – the argument of this book exactly – but also to other architects' tried and tested solutions: a problem of privacy solved by reference to this masterpiece, a dilemma over internal lighting by reference to another. The genealogy of this sort of architecture–urban compromise – is so confused as to be almost impossible to define, unlike the model villa of chapter 1, structural solutions (chapter 2) and the organic house (chapter 3). Ironically, that tendency also makes urban compromise the most up-to-date of these chapters, that confusion reflecting architecture's post-modern state.

Mecanoo
House with studio

Kralingse, Rotterdam, The Netherlands, 1989–91

Mies van der Rohe, from his German pavilion in Barcelona (1929) through to the Farnsworth house (1946-50), showed how the pursuit of transparency necessarily involved radical changes to more traditional concepts of domestic space or lifestyle. Shinichi Ogawa's house goes some way towards its logical conclusion (see page 94), veering more towards the principle than the practical. The house designed by Erick van Egeraat and Francine Houben, two partners of Mecanoo, for themselves, finds a better balance.

Their house has to be more than just a statement of their practice style, accommodating several distinctly utilitarian requirements such as children and a studio for working at home. Their greatest compromise is the balance between a house open to all views and the means to enjoy average privacy within the density of a modern city. The conflict creates a remarkably transparent house, though one made habitable by devices several decades removed from Miesian dogma.

Their struggle is certainly made worthwhile by the location. The Kralingse Plas, a spectacular lake on the edge of Rotterdam, lies to the north of the house across a far-from-busy main road of typical Dutch brick houses. A small canal stretches away to the south and the centre of the city, the back gardens of nineteenth-century, pitched-roof houses running down to its banks. Ducks crash-land into the canal as if directed on to an aqueous

The north-facing street façade of the House with studio. The architects, Mecanoo, manage to achieve a sensible compromise between sufficiently large windows to enjoy the view of the lake opposite and a sense of privacy.

A double-height space, protected from the sun by a bamboo screen, rises through the upper two levels (opposite). The device allows the family to maintain constant contact between the library (right) and the living room below.

runway by the control tower of a nearby airport.

The beauty of the views and the layout of existing buildings suggested a house placed parallel to the main road and as tall as its neighbours. Such urban good manners, however, would have condemned one half of the house to a constant northern aspect, while the southern elevation would have been left exposed to the full intensity of the sun. The climatic problems would have been worsened by the level of glazing proposed for the house – one side would have been too cold, the other too hot. The architects' solution was to organize the house in such a way that the interior was largely one volume. Any 'room', therefore, enjoyed an equal division of views and light.

The success of this solution can be seen in section. The main rooms are placed on the first and second floors: three bedrooms and a study above a living room, dining area and a kitchen. The two levels are intimately connected by a double-height space rising above the dining table. This device leaves the family in constant communication: an adult in the study can look down at children eating at the table below; the bedrooms become a continuous circular route round the void. Historically, the section also recalls Chareau's Maison de Verre (1928-31) where the open-deck access to the bedrooms also overlooks the sitting room below. Coincidentally, van Egeraat and Houben place magazines on the balustrade, just

Traditional rooms, as such, do not really exist. Free-standing walls provide the only proper division between different areas of activities, as in the kitchen.

like Chareau's arrangement of books around the edge of the great double-height sitting room of the Maison de Verre.

These architects break fundamentally with Chareau's means of achieving privacy, however, avoiding the great opaque glass wall of the Maison de Verre. Van Egeraat and Houben instead choose a variety of methods. First, the order of rooms. Philip Johnson's own Glass house in New Canaan, Connecticut (1949), achieves transparency with a simple glass box. The only privacy is created by a central brick cylinder containing the bathroom. Johnson, heavily criticized for the sheer nudity of his own house, fought back with the Wiley house, also in New Canaan (1953). A massive sitting room was placed over bedroom and bathrooms on the ground floor; a glass pavilion floating over an almost-blind masonry podium below. The contrast between private and public domains could scarcely have been more strongly made.

Van Egeraat and Houben try something similar, but, where Johnson sought to divide the two zones horizontally, the Dutch architects attempt something less clear cut. The two upper levels of living quarters are placed over a ground-floor garage and studio. The garage, with its four-panelled sliding door, creates a solid podium below the two levels of the glazed pavilion above. The rear elevation, however, is an altogether more complicated affair.

The ground-floor studio, a room usually found on the top floor of architects' houses where it benefits from the best light, suffers little loss of light as its position is compensated for by a huge window on to the garden. The rest of the façade is partially glazed, but wood panels of composite blocks obscure where necessary – the stairs between studio and kitchen, for example, and the bathroom between the parents' and children's bedrooms are hidden. The distinction between opaque and transparent blocks builds up into a tableau, expressing the interior as an arrangement of different, quite unequal, parts.

The architects continue their differentiation of the three façades with the partially solid concrete and partially glazed side façade. The whole wall is dominated by a double-height metal frame, covered in bamboo rods, which can be hydraulically drawn across the window as a screen against the sun and prying eyes. Even the street façade, the most pure of all three, has a vertical screen mounted up one side, its rear downlit by natural light shining through a hole in the overhanging roof.

Van Egeraat and Houben's decision to treat each façade differently has allowed them to create a family house that is habitable in the city. Their method is far from decorative, but combines the modern movement's principled sacrifice of comfort and a later era's interest in habitability.

At present, the house sits beside an empty development site. But, even when that is filled and despite its architectural vocabulary, this house will still fit sympathetically into a street of typical Dutch houses.

The south façade looks onto
the neighbour's back
gardens and a small canal.

Floor plans (left to right):
ground floor, garden, studio
and garage; first floor, living
room and kitchen; second
floor, bedrooms and library.

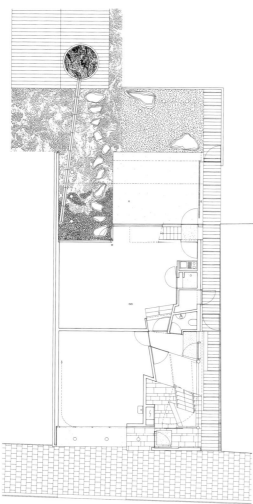

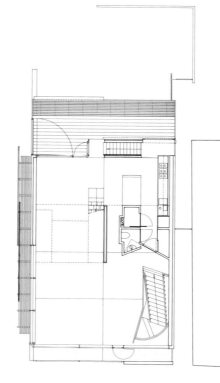

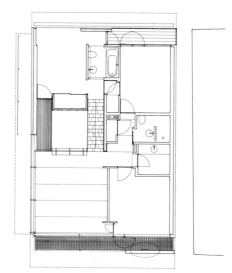

Ground floor   First floor   Second floor

David Wild
42 and 44 Rochester Place

Camden Town, London, UK, 1977 and 1989

42 Rochester Place (right) was designed and built after the completion of the earlier 44 (left). In designing the pair, Wild is suggesting a possible and infinitely replicable prototype for living within the city.

Few architects get to design two adjoining buildings in a city. David Wild did, creating first 44 Rochester Place for himself and then, when that was complete (1984), building a larger house for a client on a plot next door. Both houses have common characteristics: they each have rendered exteriors, each is dominated by a concrete column; and both their street façades are punctured by big *piano nobile* windows which let light into interiors dominated by their first-floor, double-height living rooms.

Of course, there are differences: the compact and overlapping interior spaces of the smaller number 44 contrast with the luxurious finishes and axial circulation of number 42; the flat roof, terrace and top-floor studio of number 44 give way to the shallow, pyramidal roof of number 42. What matters, though, is not how Wild develops one theme over a ten-year period as much as how he makes one strong vocabulary work for two different houses, for any house in the city is something of a compromise.

The two houses sit in a quiet street opposite Reed's Place, a pedestrianized precinct of nineteenth-century terrace houses. Both houses respond to this environment with basic urban good manners: the parapet level continues that set by the older houses; the render of the new houses is the ironed-out equivalent of the nearby banded Victorian stucco; number 44 occupies just two-thirds of its site, like many traditional north

London houses. Wild was forced to manoeuvre the buildings' footprint by the local planning authority's stipulation that an existing poplar tree be preserved. A car port and number 44's single-storey bathroom block allowed its roots to breathe. Unfortunately, the tree subsequently died and it had to be replaced.

Wild's response to the area also enriches the brief. The best view, for example, is down Reed's Place. The architect manipulates the geometry of the street elevations so that neither building is forced to look on to the blank end walls of the nearest houses. Number 44 achieves this by placing the main window at the corner, neatly emphasizing its intentionally asymmetrical façade. Number 42's symmetrical façade, however, is upset by the main window being placed off-centre to catch the view. A slightly recessed grey-painted panel attempts to restore the lost symmetry.

Views out must be balanced with issues of privacy, and those huge windows are made practicable by their first-floor position. Invasion by prying eyes would only be possible through the most extreme effort. The interiors, though, are bathed in natural light and enjoy all the benefits of the view on to Reed's Place. The rear façades do much the same, co-opting the neighbouring back gardens as numbers 42 and 44's own property. Wild is left to place secondary bedrooms and bathrooms on the ground floor of both houses,

Street elevation (above) and garden elevation (below) of 44 and 42 Rochester Place. Unfortunately the tree between the two died, although another one is rapidly growing to replace it.

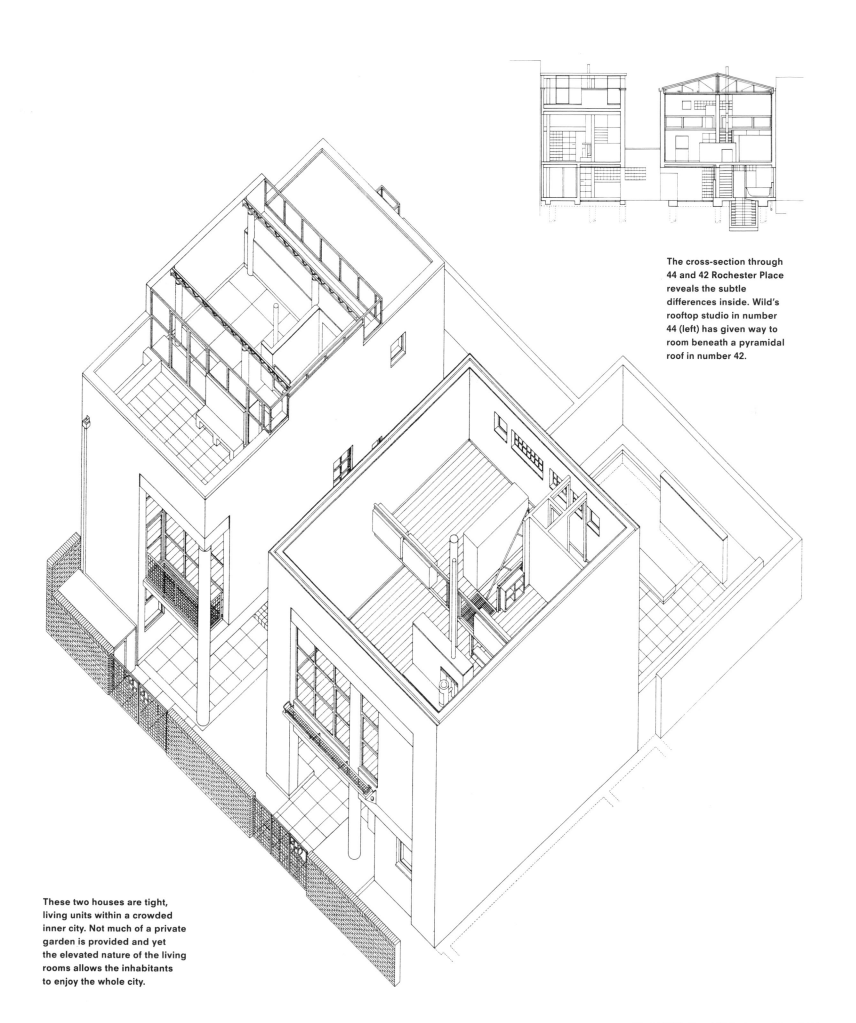

The cross-section through 44 and 42 Rochester Place reveals the subtle differences inside. Wild's rooftop studio in number 44 (left) has given way to room beneath a pyramidal roof in number 42.

These two houses are tight, living units within a crowded inner city. Not much of a private garden is provided and yet the elevated nature of the living rooms allows the inhabitants to enjoy the whole city.

The plan and circulation routes in number 42 follow a formal, axial arrangement at odds with the more compact geometries of number 44. The view from the front door (above) is terminated by the stair that leads to the main living floor (right). A lighter, steel stair leads up again to a gallery (left).

The compact nature of number 44 is mitigated by constantly opening views across and through the living space (left and below). David Wild's own studio occupies the upper floor (right).

their privacy and daylight preserved by glass bricks. The ground-floor location is, however, far from second best, with bedrooms opening on to the walled back gardens.

Yet, Wild's empathy, forced or otherwise, conveniently shadows his own agenda. Modernism, to him, is a style, one reminiscent of heroic socialism. The two houses, in that sense, are somewhat old-fashioned, hangovers from the inter-war decades of modernist house building. Number 44 is a hybrid of Le Corbusier's Maison Citrohan and theoretical Dom-ino house: there is the loadbearing façade around an *in situ* concrete frame; the corner column can be read as a *piloti*; and the section with its dog-leg staircase is resolved in a roof-top garden terrace. Wild fulfils three of Le Corbusier's 'five points' from the 1920s, one fewer than Tadao Ando (see page 65). What updates them here is Wild's intellectual and philosophical interests.

Wild sees himself as a rationalist on the lines of continental Europe, rather than a modernist. The façades can therefore be reinterpreted as reflecting the concerns of the past two decades, not just those of 60 years ago. The corner columns and recessed window of number 44 compare to the Dickes house of Rob Krier (1974–76); the pyramidal roof above the symmetry of number 42 recalls a theoretical public loggia by Leon Krier; and Wild's respectful relationship with the existing city fits firmly within recent European ideology, contrasting with the

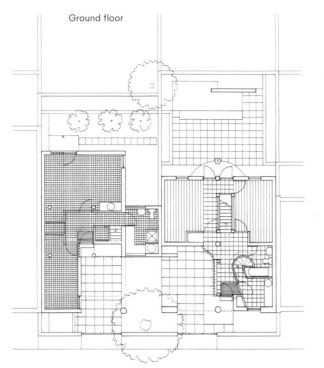

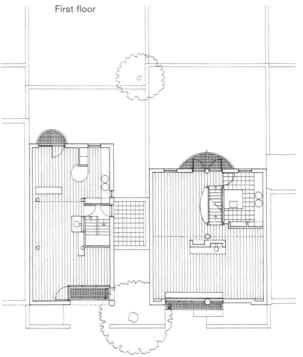

Floor plans (left to right): street level, entrances and utlity; first floor, living rooms and kitchens; second floor, bedrooms; third floor, Wild's studio. The exterior of 42 Rochester Place (below right).

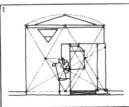

The complex range of influences on number 44, Rochester Place, include Le Corbusier's Maison Citrohan (above) and the Dickes house of Rob Krier (left).

rather more grandiose urban concepts of the modern era such as Le Corbusier's 'La ville radieuse' (1930). Number 44, for example, is an urban prototype which could easily become a double villa or be multiplied to form a city terrace.

What finally modernizes the two houses is Wild's approach to construction. Just as he equates modernism with style – an iconoclastic connection for an architectural form supposedly informed by function or social purpose – so he ignores the myth of machine-age modernism. First, Le Corbusier's Maison Citrohan, despite the pun on the car manufacturer Citroën, were, in fact, custom-built one-offs, more expensive and more difficult to build than any other house at the 1927 Weißenhofsiedlung in Stuttgart. That contrast between the so-called *machine à habiter* and the reality of craftsmanship required to create modernist aesthetics has caused two generations of angst, something that has not affected Wild.

Second, the development in the technology of the early twentieth century allowed the types of constructional methods which made modernism possible. But much of the technology was not up to the job, providing the form but not the function: hence, Le Corbusier's leaking roofs, Mies van der Rohe's freezing-cold rooms, and so on. Wild sees construction technology as finally catching up with a 60-year-old style. Pure white walls are now possible with modern renders which

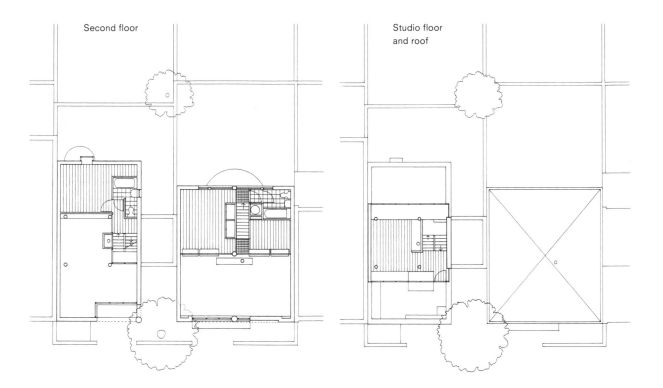

Second floor

Studio floor
and roof

do not crack; aerated concrete blocks are easy to cut, creating the desired abstract form; higher standard finishes for metal windows make them wind- and rain-proof; and metal deck roofs, requiring minimal support, make flat roofs desirable. Technology has finally caught up with the modern style.

Studio Granda
Haus im Vordertaunus

Wiesbaden, Germany, 1989–92

A noisy road, a view, the sun's orientation; these were some of the factors that led Studio Granda to separate the house into main and guest blocks, the space in between providing a little, private courtyard, away from the road, though filled with sun.

A competition creates the notion that there must be fewer restrictions on a building than for a straight commission. Competitors, after all, boast a whole range of styles suggesting that any one of them would be suitable. Such a process would be ideal for a green-field site without any neighbours. But the city or the suburb has no such freedom; each and every house is influenced by the nature of its location.

The clients, therefore, must be commended for the generosity of their commission. When the family decided to give up the pleasures of their cramped, inner-city apartment in favour of the suburbs, they found, through a competition, Studio Granda – an Iceland-based practice comprising Margrét Hardardóttir and Steve Christer. Such a method, though fraught with problems in many countries, is more common in Germany, where public buildings of any size are open to competition. The family's decision, therefore, was far from radical, though it is still unusual for a private client.

What is surprising is the scale of the family's ambition. A group of young architects from around the world was asked to participate, handpicked by mentors who included Tadao Ando, Rafael Moneo, Luigi Snozzi, Jean Nouvel, Robert Venturi and Peter Cook. The participants were then given a brief, set by one of the five judges, Dalibor Vesely, a theorist and teacher at Cambridge

The two blocks (opposite and right) have names. The wooden, lighter building is the House of Delia while the House of Saturn is darker and brooding. The names are a reference to the theme of the competition brief – an obscure, medieval text.

University. He suggested that the competition theme should revolve around the *Hypnerotomachia Poliphili*, a late fifteenth-century fable by the Italian monk Francesco Colonna.

The tale tells the story of a young man, Polifilo, who, seeking his lover Polia in the forest, comes upon some ancient ruins. The subtext portrays a dreamer on the look-out for truth in an era of instability and uncertainty. Studio Granda's most obvious response to the allegorical nature of the brief emphasized one aspect of the fable in particular: Polifilo recounts how Polia was expelled from the home of the goddess Delia, causing his search to begin.

The architects felt that this incident best summed up the hero's character because, in the telling of the story, his confusion and desire for self-realization become clear. The architects split the building into two parts. The main building became the House of Delia: their reasoning being that the home should be a constant source of security for a growing family, and Delia, after all, sent Polia down that path by forcing her to face the world. The smaller part, by contrast, became the House of Saturn, Delia's polar opposite, a dark, brooding presence. The final planning for the site can also be explained by other, more mundane, reasons, such as urban compromise and family lifestyles.

The clients were explicit in their demands for specific spaces, such as a cupboard for gardening

The flight of stairs (left) leading up to the roof of the House of Delia lies behind the wooden façade and between the glazed wall of the access corridor to the bedrooms on the upper level of the house.

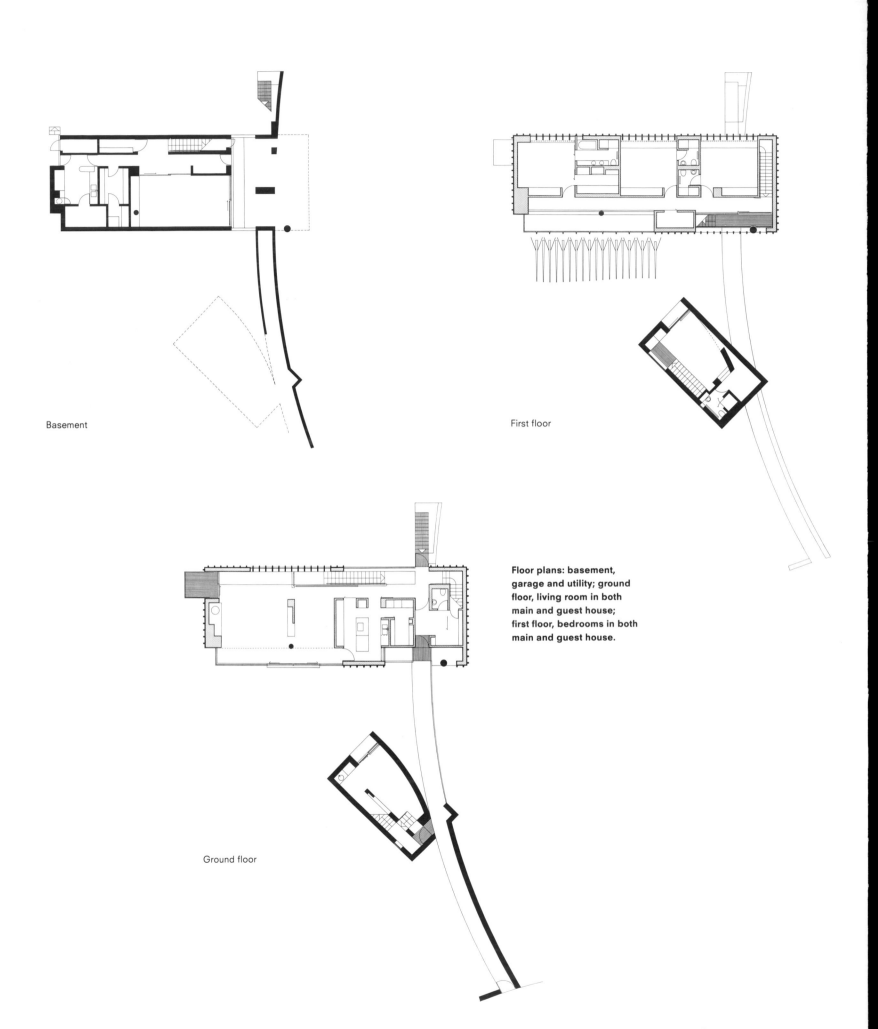

Basement

First floor

Ground floor

Floor plans: basement, garage and utility; ground floor, living room in both main and guest house; first floor, bedrooms in both main and guest house.

The wooden louvres of the main block (right) create something of a house within a house – the complexity of an everyday domestic environment is scarcely expressed by the simplicity of the exterior.

tools and a bike store. Each member of the family was also clear on the relationship between individual rooms. Most importantly, the site was off a road and beside orchards and a steep, wooded ravine. The family were keen to cut themselves off from the adjacent and occasionally busy road while benefitting from the view of nearby countryside.

Merely orienting the building away from the road and over the valley condemned the house to constant north light. Studio Granda therefore broke down the house into two parts: the small guest house (or the House of Saturn) standing defensively between the road and the larger family house (the House of Delia) standing beside the ravine. The space in between the two houses becomes a semi-private courtyard and gives an alternative view of the ravine.

Studio Granda's strategy allows one house, which is, in fact, two buildings, to take on different forms and appearances. The guest house mimics the pitched roofs of the suburban neighbours, while rewriting the rules with red rendered walls and lead roof. The main house is a rectangle covered in red cedar strips and laths. Huge windows are cut into the simple volume, those on the south protected from the summer sun by an arbour of vines. The two houses also neatly divide the activities of the household.

The smaller building accommodates a guest suite above a study and library, all functions that work best with an element of privacy and detachment from a lively family. The bigger building also has bedrooms at first-floor level reached off a single corridor, with garage, store rooms and laundry in the basement. The living rooms are at ground-floor level, often running the full width of the house to enjoy sunlight on one side and the view on the other.

The obscurity of the Polifilo text can be seen as something of a red herring; the Haus im Vordertaunus, as built by Studio Granda, however, does conjure up something of the fable. There is the northern side of the house, 'darker, like Polifilo's soul'; and the wooded ravine below, through which 'he could so easily have wandered'. The larger House of Delia is 'a destination of light' and, with its arbour covered in vines, 'renewal', which is approached past the threatening mass of the House of Saturn. The imagery evoked by Studio Granda provides a little poetry to their otherwise straightforward, though skilled, planning of an awkward, arrow-head-shaped site.

Glenn Murcutt
Ken Done house

Mosman, NSW, Australia, 1988–91

Glenn Murcutt manages to create a responsible, two-storey street façade and yet the manipulation of the section exploits absolutely the change in levels across the site. The volume created inside accommodates a spectacular gallery, which is triple height at one point.

A typical house by Glenn Murcutt stands in a remote part of Australia's dramatic countryside, its barrel-vault or butterfly roof of corrugated-iron sheets rising from the Australian landscape. The Ken Done house, however, is an exception in his domestic *oeuvre*. First, the house sits in a suburb of Sydney which, although attractive, presents Murcutt with far more of a challenge to achieve the qualities of privacy, view and light possible in the wild. Second, this is his first masonry construction. The Done house suggests that Murcutt has accommodated his more usual style to the city.

Murcutt's early houses were a series of Miesian pavilions in glass and steel, such as the Laurie Short house in the Terrey Hills (1972). But a visit to several American modern movement classics in the early 1970s raised doubts about the environmental suitability of such structures. Gradually, while retaining the rationalism of the plan and the clarity of construction, he developed the basic pavilion until the houses boasted their own identity.

The best examples of Murcutt's vision are the Ball & Eastway house, Glenorie (1983), and the Magney house, Bingie Point (1984). The barrel-vault of one and the butterfly roof of the other, both in corrugated-iron sheets placed above the louvred, glazed walls, set up Murcutt's trademark. The departure from the rationalism of the Miesian section and elevation was also a desire to respond more closely to the landscape, both in the

The central courtyard is a device common to much contemporary domestic architecture since it allows for a delightful level of privacy and calm within the bustle of today's cities. But the skill lies in ensuring that the device is truly part of the house, as in the Done house where all the major spaces are separated only by glass.

The barrel-vault of the Ball & Eastway house at Glenorie (far left) and the butterfly roof of the Magney house at Bingie Point (left).

The garage with a roof-terrace on the street which runs behind the site. This building is one and two levels higher than the main front façade. The small gate is also a public entrance to the gallery.

Theoretically the Done house appears to have little in common with Murcutt's other houses, with their barrel-vault or butterfly roofs. But, in reality, this house picks up on the ideas the architect has been developing for his more recent and more urban projects such as the Magney house, Paddington (1990).

appearance of the exterior and to the climatic and contextual advantage of the interior, as Murcutt has always sought an indigenous Australian architecture.

This land is making the new culture of Australia. This country will eventually make us; we won't make it, Murcutt has said. He looks to the outback for inspiration, with its rugged trees covered in delicate silver leaves growing in scorched earth. He also cites aboriginal traditions as a way of dwelling. For them to be able to see the sky, to see who's coming, who's going, what weather patterns are occurring, is very important, he says. So, a typical Murcutt house has services and circulation kept to a zone at the rear, opening up an enfilade of living and bedrooms to the view and verandas. Overhangs from the roof shelter the walls from the sun, while breezes cool the interior.

Murcutt has kept to these rules even for his few city houses. The Littlemore house, Woollhara (1986), is oriented to make an adjacent town park appear like a front garden, its living rooms placed to take maximum advantage of the rare city view. Its façade is another composition of glass and louvres within a steel frame. And the Magney house, Paddington (1990), converts a nineteenth-century terrace house into one great viewing platform of a nearby wooded hillside, a dramatically contrasting panorama compared with its inner-city location. But the Ken Done house, displaying some generic features, has sufficient novelty to suggest that the architect has

developed with this commission a vocabulary for the city distinct from this earlier design, both for his rural and earlier urban work.

There is enough, though, that has kept Murcutt to this customary path. The client, for example, fits neatly into Murcutt's search for an authentic Australian culture. Done, like Laura Ashley in Britain or Hermès in France, is a fabric designer whose exuberantly coloured products efficiently distil the essence of his country. The location in Chinaman's Bay has not escaped from the tract-like houses more often seen in Australian soap opera. Yet, heavily wooded slopes around the bay of sandy beaches still create a site nearly as beautiful as those enjoyed by the outback houses. Murcutt, however, has chosen here to move his architecture forward.

The house is surrounded by an almost-solid masonry wall to provide maximum privacy. Rooms overlook a small, central courtyard, providing an intimate focus for the inhabitants not dissimilar to the approach taken by Tadao Ando (see page 70). The layout, therefore, contrasts with Murcutt's other buildings, placing more emphasis on views within the building footprint than of the world outside. The courtyard creates a quality of introversion not seen elsewhere in Murcutt's work. The exterior louvres and blue, stainless-steel drainwater pipes, are the only hint at Murcutt's structural aesthetics seen in previous projects.

Floor plans (from top): street level, main entrance and bedrooms; first floor, living room, courtyard and main bedroom; second floor, upper street entrance and garage; third floor, roof terrace, butterfly roof over gallery and barrel vault roof over living room.

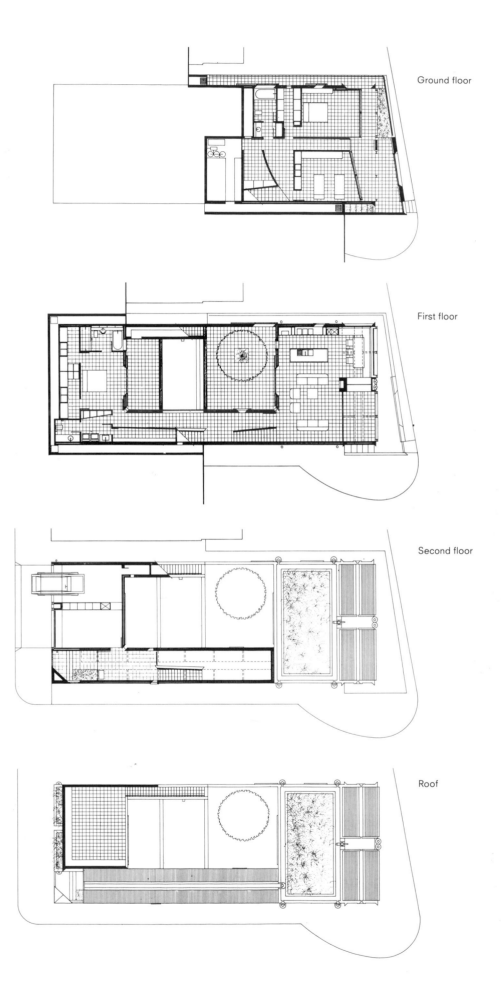

Ground floor

First floor

Second floor

Roof

Walls, instead, are rendered blocks. Their solidity is not a necessary response to an awkward sloping site – Mies van der Rohe's Tugendhat villa in Brno (1930) showed how to deal with such a location – but a means of obscuring prying eyes in a way that a Miesian pavilion with its glass walls would find impossible.

Murcutt has solved some of the problems in familiar ways and even the new introversion and masonry construction have precedents. The main floor of the house is carved into the sloping site, leaving living/dining rooms, courtyard and parents' bedroom all on one level. The children's bedrooms are then hidden away below and the garage is secreted above. The circulation zone is kept to one strip, just like in those pavilion houses, but this time Murcutt exploits the site to create a staircase/gallery that, almost triple-height at one point, is ideal for the larger canvases of Done's extensive collection of modern paintings.

Windows are kept to a minimum, except towards the sea and through to the courtyard, so that the client has maximum wall space for hanging. Light, instead, comes through roof-lights on rib-like arches over the stairs, dining room and veranda. Electronically controlled aluminium louvres cover the roof-lights, their butterfly-shaped forms either side of a rain gully, reminiscent, on a smaller scale, of Murcutt's roof treatment of the Magney house on Bingie Point. And the long

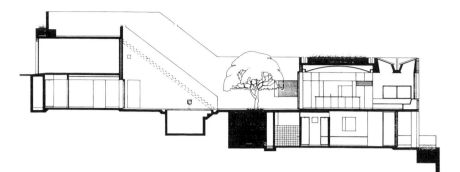

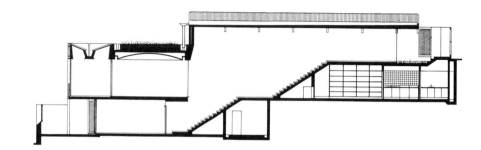

Long sections. Main rooms are kept to one level, despite the change in level across the site (left) and yet the location's very character provides the opportunity for the flight of stairs/triple-height gallery.

The blank street wall, which rises across the site, provides the space for Done's extensive modern art collection. Views to the right are of the peaceful courtyard.

barrel-vault over the sitting room/kitchen takes Murcutt back to his earlier vision.

Even the courtyard has some consistency with Murcutt's earlier work. The house in Paddington has a garden running between two red rendered walls, its paved surface broken by still pools of water. The Done House courtyard has a similar pool, but develops the garden theme with a waterspout and the clear treads of the stairs up to the roof terrace above the garage. The composition, like Pawson and Silvestrin's Neuendorf house (see page 34), recalls the work of Luis Barragán, and, like Pawson and Silvestrin, the reference is a device for authentic architecture appropriated to the city.

Hajime Yatsuka
Yatsuka residence

Komae, Tokyo, Japan, 1987–88

The generator for Hajime Yatsuka's house, as for many of his Japanese contemporaries, is the density of Japanese cities. Tadao Ando's houses, for example, have come to be seen as something of a classic answer to such a problem, as with the Kidosaki house (see page 66), which is turned into a self-contained unit within the city. Even the outside environment is transformed into carefully selected compositions framed by the building itself. Such ideas, though built in concrete and glass, are set deeply within the traditions of Japanese domestic architecture.

The Komae house also acknowledges its context. Yatsuka thinks that 'houses are impossible to complete as a whole' in Japanese cities, where plots are simply too small to leave houses standing grandly detached as is the Western ideal. Instead, a house does and, more importantly for Yatsuka, can appear as one or two houses both in form and style: 'This kind of poly-style is rather popular in contemporary architecture because it is a reflection of the most basic condition of the contemporary city, whether in the west or in Japan,' he says.

Yatsuka's house, therefore, comes with two, not one, references to historic examples of houses: a bit of Le Corbusier's Maisons La Roche and Jeanneret (1923–25) and the fin de siècle style of Vienna. His urban rule, like Ando's, recognizes the Japanese past while adapting modernism to the Japanese

While the L-shaped plan and the garden façade of the Yatsuka residence recall Le Corbusier's Maisons La Roche and Jeanneret, the street façade is treated like a screen through which the house is entered.

The Yatsuka residence is informed by both practical and theoretical ideals. The L-shaped plan cuts the garden off from the adjacent road. The two wings divide the more public activities of the living quarters from the more private nature of the bedrooms, accommodating each in their own wing. Most importantly, the two parts provide Hajime Yatsuka with an opportunity to create what he calls a 'poly-style'.

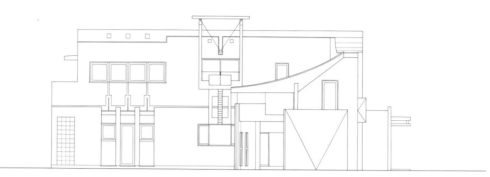

The interior (left) and exterior (below) of the living/dining room. Inside, the space is double-height, while the curve of the exterior is a contrasting combination of curved wall and window, over which the roof appears to float.

condition. But Yatsuka's agenda, expressed in a variety of styles, unlike Ando's doctrinaire form, has a harder task to gain legitimacy within a modernist framework.

The modernist house, often purely an intellectual statement or a reaction to the previous century's domestic architecture, rarely expressed more than one idea. Such purity is scarcely able to accommodate today's diversity. The post-modern condition has partly liberated architecture from these rules, and Yatsuka's experience acknowledges this change. He was a student of Kenzo Tange, who sought to find a Japanese identity for architecture within the massive changes of post-war society.

Yatsuka was then appointed project architect for Arata Isozaki's Los Angeles Museum of Contemporary Art. Isozaki is an architect who has gloried in architecture as a process of constant change; both he and Tange provided Yatsuka with visible legitimacy for a diversity of styles, though this has developed largely as a process of layering, not too distantly removed from deconstruction. Yatsuka, of course, would deny it: 'My aim is not to give something novel, something shocking, like deconstructivist design, just to avoid homogeneity.' What he has sought since is his own intellectual justification.

'The Komae house is fragmented, owing to the condition of the site and the programme,' says Yatsuka. An L-shaped layout turns one wing

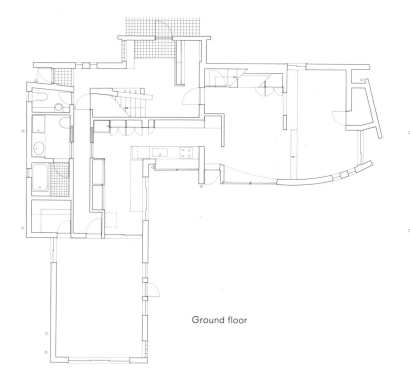

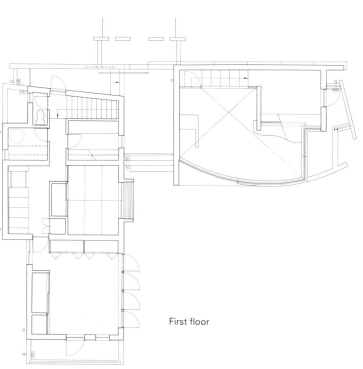

Ground floor

First floor

Floor plans. Although making reference to Corbusier's Maisons La Roche and Jeanneret, Yatsuka reverses the L-shaped floor plan for reasons of privacy.

towards the neighbouring properties, the other towards the garden. Each one has its own appearance. The street elevation is treated like an appliqué or a screen, an intention made explicit when it is viewed end on. Yatsuka describes it as 'an autonomous façade which does not let you anticipate the state of things behind'. The other façade, meanwhile, turns the house towards the garden. The composition makes one 'façade belong to the outer world, while a back body belongs to the family'.

The garden side presents the first image of the house as a whole, but Yatsuka breaks this down even further into public/private zones: the wing behind the entrance façade contains the living/dining room, with a studio on a mezzanine; the other wing contains the master bedroom, children's room and Tatami room. Such separation is not unusual for a private home, unlike Yatsuka's means of expressing the interior.

Yatsuka kept the L-shaped plan of Le Corbusier's La Roche-Jeanneret house in mind during the design process of his own house (though he reversed it in the final plan). More specifically, the curved wall used by Le Corbusier is repeated in the plan of the living/dining wing. The sleeping wing, by contrast, boasts references to the Viennese architecture of Otto Wagner and Josef Hoffmann.

He explains his choice as one of 'private preferences rather than references'. The

The sleeping wing of the Yatsuka residence displays references to Josef Hoffmann's Palais Stoclet (1905–11).

living/dining room is a place in which visitors are received and is therefore more formal than the sleeping wing. Yatsuka sees a modern expression of such activities as more appropriate. 'The *machine à habiter* was a device to enhance the spirit of people living in it,' he says. He believes that the Viennese masters offer a more homely image for the sleeping wing, with the 'greater hedonism of their private lives and more understanding of *Gemütlichkeit*'.

The composition of the Komae house with its two wings around a garden achieves the same end result as Ando's courtyards – both enjoy a level of privacy unusual in Japanese cities – but they speak in architectural languages distantly removed from each other. Ando's houses are a moment of tranquil peace from frenetic activity; Yatsuka sees contemporary lifestyles as 'composed of dual states of things and mind', and therefore he tries to reflect the reality of today more accurately, if less poetically.

Allies and Morrison
Oakyard

The Keep, Blackheath, London, UK, 1991–93

The planning restrictions imposed on Oakyard, though severe, were far from awkward for its architects Allies and Morrison. The house stands between several Span estates – a series of post-war private housing developments filling the gaps between Blackheath's huge Victorian villas – which have offered relatively cheap modern homes to a generation of families.

The success of Span rested with the architect Eric Lyons, who offered each householder small, private back gardens in return for the large, communal space in between. This environment provided a sense of spaciousness and grandeur that went way beyond the relative cheapness of the houses. For, in essence, a Span home was a typical, post-war, modern terrace house, though better built than its contemporaries.

Graham Morrison, of Allies and Morrison, was intimately involved with the Span programme. He worked for Lyons between 1977 and 1980, and even lived in one of the houses. When a plot of land came up on the edge of one development in 1980, Morrison snapped it up, biding his time until he could afford to build his own home. He set up his own practice in 1984 with Bob Allies, and has developed an architectural language that helps to explain Oakyard and Morrison's lack of a problem with context.

Much British post-war architecture has developed differently from the sort of structural

At first glance, Oakyard appears to be just like any other suburban British house. Picking up on some of the traditional elements of nearby Victorian villas and the post-war vernacular of the adjacent Span estates by Eric Lyons, the architects have taken these clichés as a starting-point for a subtle, though honest, modern architecture.

Modern British vernacular. Alison and Peter Smithson's Sugden house (1956) with its asymmetrical expression of interior organization.

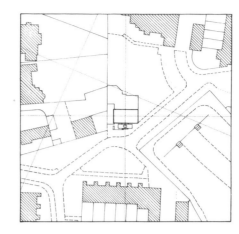

Site plan. The success of the Span estates relied on some personal sacrifice for the good of the whole community; small private gardens and grand, communal spaces.

logic that is suggested by the public and international reputations of Sir Norman Foster or Sir Richard Rogers. More typical is a form of building which tries to marry the vernacular to modernism. The housing of James Stirling and James Gowan in the 1950s – such as the flats at Ham Common (1955–58) or the house at Cowes (1956) – are good examples where a traditional British use of brickwork is wrapped around a more contemporary approach to space and volume.

But a better example, perhaps, is the Sugden house at Watford by Alison and Peter Smithson (1956). The exterior looks much like any other suburban house, with its second-hand London stock bricks and pitched roof, but the interior is very different. Another glance at the exterior reveals the asymmetry of the elevation, the size and distribution of windows relating directly to the rooms inside.

Allies and Morrison's practice has deliberately continued this vernacular tradition from the 1950s. Their work pays particular attention to the problems of inserting new uses into established contexts, creating an architecture that is rational, though far from prototypical. Morrison sees their theme as 'a language trying to bring modernism into our culture'. Oakyard's necessary urban compromise is, therefore, rather different for these architects than for many others: first, contextualism is always the basis of their approach

Living and dining rooms run into each other, both opening onto a patio and the garden. This reliance on modern, domestic planning is the key to both Oakyard and the earlier Sugden house – a contemporary approach to space and volume within a familiar architectural vocabulary.

and, second, the location suggests exactly the kind of architecture that interests them.

Oakyard picks up on many of the features common to Lyons' Span housing. The house is in brick, though, and has a pitched roof, rather than a flat roof like the earlier Span houses. The entrance porch stands out from the rest of the building perimeter. The adjacent public open space, in time-honoured Span tradition, appears as part of Oakyard's own extensive grounds running

Floor plans: ground floor,
open plan living room;
first floor, four bedrooms.

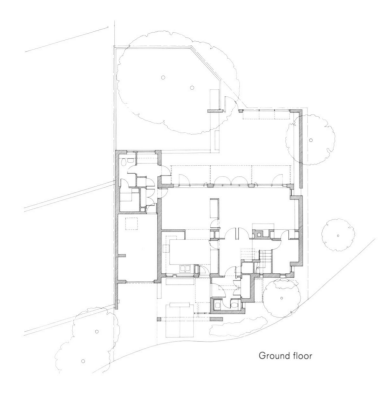

Ground floor

First floor

out from what is, in reality, the small private garden. Each element is just sufficiently innovative to underline the difference between a one-off house and a terrace, suggesting further comparisons with the Sugden house.

The walls and roof of the building, for all their traditional appearance, have been dealt with in a modernist fashion – not as mere solids but as planes. The white, rendered entrance can be read as a reference to the Victorian villas nearby. This feature can also be seen in Allies and Morrison's more mainstream work such as the Scott Howard building (1990) in Islington, where the concept of buildings within buildings (Oakyard's entrance porch also contains a bathroom) is made clear; the white render of the interior walls comes through to be part of the exterior façade.

Another 'layer' is the roof: it is pitched but is expressed as a wafer-thin cap to the house, flying over the two ends of the house as a cantilever.

Morrison suggests that the nature of the front and back façades is primarily determined by environmental factors: the north façade has small windows and minimal exposure to the winter winds; the south has as much glazing as possible to absorb the winter sun. The two elevations, however, like the Sugden house, also express the interior, where living and dining rooms are located towards the south, and bathrooms, kitchen and stairs are kept towards the north. Family rooms

evidently need bigger windows than those for services, so the southern façade, with its many windows, is far more open than the northern façade, which has a greater ration of brick to glass.

Oakyard's similarities to the Sugden house continue inside as both have an L-shaped, ground-floor living space. Oakyard's open ground-floor plan centres round a loadbearing wall/chimney, which can be compartmentalized into a series of individual rooms with the doors closed, transformed into a circulation route with the doors open, or, most dramatically, open directly on to the small garden patio. Upstairs, the bedrooms are the same; either four traditional rooms or, with the doors pivoted back, one open space.

A final similarity between the two houses rests with a certain sort of Englishness. The Smithsons' super-rationalism meant that the Sugden house has no suspended ceiling; ground-floor rooms have exposed beams; and the upper bedrooms stretch into the void of the pitched roof. Ironically, the architects' obsession has created an interior similar to a thousand English weekend cottages. Allies and Morrison are more frank. Doors throughout Oakyard follow a hierarchy; oak-veneered for the main rooms downstairs, vertical panels for the upstairs bedrooms, and plain panels for cupboards and bathrooms. The rustic feel of the Sugden house is translated into the equally British ideal of Allies and Morrison's arts and crafts suggestions.

Further reading

ALLIES, Bob, & MORRISON, Graham
Swenarton, Mark. 'Allies and Morrison Architects: Oakyard, The Keep, Blackheath, London'. *The art of the process: architectural design in practice*, edited by Louise Rogers. Exhibition catalogue produced by the Royal Institute of British Architects. London: The Builder Group, 1993.

ANDO, Tadao
Frampton, Kenneth. *Tadao Ando*. New York: Museum of Modern Art, 1991.

BEEL, Stéphane
Welsh, John. 'Class Walls'. *RIBA Journal*, 100(9), 1993.

BOTTA, Mario
dal Co, Francesco. *Mario Botta*. London: Architectural Press, 1985.
Frampton, Kenneth. *Mario Botta*. London: Academy Editions, 1981.
Frampton, Kenneth. 'Botta's paradigm'. *Progressive Architecture*, December 1984.
Wrede, Stuart. *Mario Botta*. New York: MOMA, 1986.

CAMPO BAEZA, Alberto
Zabalbeascoa, Anatxu. *The New Spanish Architecture*. New York: Rizzoli, 1992.
Baeza, Alberto Campa. 'True white'. *Baumeister*, December 1991.
Croset, Pierre-Alain. 'Three schools in Madrid'. *Casabella*, March 1987.
Baeza, Alberto Campa. 'Alberto Campo Baeza'. *L'Architecture D'Aujourd'hui*, April 1991.

DEWES, Ada & PUENTE, Sergio
Anderton, Frances. 'Jungle House'. *Architectural Review*, June 1991.
Sudjic, Deyan. 'Patina Latina'. *The World of Interiors*, February 1993.
'Monumentalidad en lo cotidiano'. *Architectural houses*, Vol. 6. Barcelona: Atrium, 1992.

GEHRY, Frank
Steele, James. *Schnabel House*. London: Phaidon Press, 1993.
Viladas, Pilar. 'Outdoor sculpture'. *Progressive Architecture*, December 1987.
Viladas, Pilar. 'House(s) on the lakeside'. *Progressive Architecture*, December 1989.

De GEYTER, Xaveer
Welsh, John. 'Class Walls'. *RIBA Journal*, 100(9), 1993.

JACKSON, Daryl
Jackson, Daryl. *Daryl Jackson: Architecture, drawings and photographs*. London: Macmillan, 1984.
Welsh, John. 'Coastal orders'. *Building Design*, 19 February, 1993.

KATSALIDIS, Nonda
Fromonot, Françoise. 'Maison de plage'. *L'Architecture d'Aujourd'hui*, February 1993.
Melhuish, Clare. *Building Design*, 26 February, 1993.
van Schaik, Leon. 'Beach houses'. *Architecture Australia*, May/June 1992.
van Schaik, Leon. 'Katsalidis towers'. *Architecture Australia*, September/October 1992.

MARSHALL, Barrie
Beck, Haig. Interview with Barrie Marshall. Melbourne: UME, 1992.
Marshall, Barrie. 'Non-evento'. *Backlogue*, Vol.1.
'Bill Corker's own house'. *Design World*, No. 18, 1990.

MECANOO
Welsh, John. 'Design menu'. *Building Design*, 22 March, 1992.
Welsh, John. 'Modern models'. *Building Design*, 24 April, 1992.

MEIER, Richard
Brawne, Michael. *Museum for Kunsthandwerk*. London: Phaidon Press, 1992.
Frampton, Kenneth and Hejduk, John. *Richard Meier 1966–76*. New York: Rizzoli, 1985.
Frampton, Kenneth and Rykwert, Joseph. *Richard Meier Architect 2*. New York: Rizzoli, 1991.
Hughes, Robert. 'Richard Meier'. *Architectural Digest*, October 1987.
Stephens, Suzanne. 'Malibu modernism'. *Progressive Architecture*, December 1987.

MIRALLES, Enric
Curtis, William J.R. *The Architecture of Enric Miralles and Carmen Pinos*. New York: Lumen, 1990.
Curtis, William J.R. 'Mapas mentales y paisajes sociales'. *El Croquis*, June/September 1991.
Welsh, John and Rattenbury, Kester. 'Paying homage to Catalonia'. *Building Design*, 23 April, 1993.
Welsh, John. 'Mi casa, es su casa'. *RIBA Journal*, 101(2), 1994.

MURCUTT, Glenn
Drew, Philip. *Leaves of iron*. North Ryde: Law Book Company, 1985.
Interview with Glenn Murcutt. 'Keeping the faith'. *Architecture Australia*, September/October 1992.
Pardey, John. 'Outback warrior'. *Building Design*, 28 April, 1989.
Sharp, Dennis 'Essence of the outback'. *Building Design*, 21 April, 1989.

OGAWA, Shinichi
Klotz, Heinrich. *The history of postmodern architecture*. Cambridge, MA: MIT Press, 1988.
Noguchi, Masao and Heneghan, Tom. *Invisible language*. London: Architectural Association, 1992.

OMA/KOOLHAAS, Rem
Fisher, Thomas. 'In the Dutch modernist tradition'. *Progressive Architecture*, December 1989.
Sudjic, Deyan. 'Tough kid on the block'. *Blueprint*, March 1992.
Wislocki, Peter. 'Kool sophistication'. *Architects' Journal*, 11 March, 1992.

PAWSON, John
Pawson, John. *John Pawson*. Introductions by Bruce Chatwin/Deyan Sudjic. Barcelona: Editorial Gustavo Gili, 1992.

PREDOCK, Antoine
Horn, Miriam. 'Antoine Predock'. *Graphis*, November/December 1991.
Lavin, Sylvia. 'Power to heal'. *Elle Decoration*, July 1990.
Stein, Karen. 'Raising Arizona'. *Architectural Record*, April 1990.

'Antoine Predock'. *L'Architecture D'Aujourd'hui*, December 1990.
Webb, Michael. 'Antoine Predock'. *Architectural Digest*, March 1992.

PRINCE, Bart
Betsky, Aaron. 'Fantastic voyage'. *Architectural Record*, April 1991.
Branch, Mark Alden. 'A breed apart'. *Progressive Architecture*, June 1992
Mead, Christopher. *Houses by Bart Prince*. Albuquerque: University of New Mexico Press, 1991
Webb, Michael. 'Of visionary nature'. *Architectural Digest*, December 1990.

SCHWEITZER, Joshua
McCabe, Christopher. 'Shifting points of view'. *Borderlines*, 1989.
Stabiner, Karen. 'Joshing around'. *Los Angeles Times Magazine*, 8 July, 1990

USHIDA, Eisaku, FINDLAY, Kathryn
Friis-Hansen, Dana. 'Truss wall house'. *Tokyo Journal*, April 1993.
Perez, Santiago. 'Slow information'. *RMIT*, Autumn/Winter, 1992.
Welsh, John. 'Interior life'. *Building Design*, 12 June, 1992.
Welsh, John. *RIBA Journal*, June 1993.

WILD, David
Wild, David. and Jenkins, David. 'A modern couple'. *Architects' Journal*, 26 April, 1989.
Wild, David. and McIntyre, Andrew. 'Self-build comes in from the wilderness'. *Architects' Journal*, 20 March, 1985.

YATSUKA, Hajime
Taki, Kaji. *Hajime Yatsuka, Architect*. Tokyo: Rikuyosha Creative Now, 1992.
Welsh, John. 'Countering clip-on culture'. *Building Design*, 4 May, 1990.

Credits

Neuendorf house
Mallorca, Spain
1987-89

Architect:
Pawson Silvestrin
27-29 Whitfield Street
London WIP 5RB
Design Team:
John Pawson
Claudio Silvestrin
Crispin Osborne
Vishwa Kaushal
Structural Engineer:
Jim Hardwick,
S B Tietz & Partners
Contractor:
Joaquin Salis Verger

Ackerberg house
Malibu, California, USA
1984-86

Architect:
Richard Meier & Partners
475 Tenth Avenue
New York, NY 10018
USA
Design Team:
Richard Meier
Steven Theodore
Marc Hacker
Mark Mascheroni
Brian Healy
Hans Li
Daniel Stuver
Client:
Norman and Lisette Ackerberg
Structural Engineer:
Severud Associates
Mechanical Engineer:
John L Altieri
General Contractor:
Ardie Tavangarian

Casa Bernasconi
Carona, Switzerland
1988-89

Architect:
Luigi Snozzi Architetto
Piazzetta dei Riformati
1-6600 Locarno
Switzerland
Collaborator:
Arch. Gustavo Groisman
Client:
A V V Raffaele Bernasconi
Structural Engineer:
Hans Peter Jenny
Contractor:
Impresa G T L

Zuber house
Paradise Valley, Phoenix,
Arizona, USA
1987-89

Architect:
Antoine Predock Architect
300 12th Street, NW
Albuquerque
New Mexico 87102
USA
Design Team:
Antoine Predock
Geoffrey Beebe
Tim Rohleder
Ronald Jacob
Jim Williams
Sam Sterling
Joe Barden
Mark Harris
Hadrian Predock

Client:
Dr and Mrs Judy Zuber
Landscape Architect:
Nancy Gerczynski
Civil Engineer:
John F Olney
Interiors:
Mitzi Vernon and Judy Zuber
Lighting:
Roger Smith
Contractor:
Saddleback Construction

Casa Gaspar
Zahora, Cadiz, Spain
1990-91

Architect:
Alberto Campo Baeza Architect
Almirante 9
28004 Madrid
Spain
Design Team:
Alberto Campo Baeza
Francisco Arevalo Toro
Client:
Gaspar Guerrero Castro
Contractor:
Manuel Romero Sanchez

Kidosaki house
Setagaya, Tokyo, Japan
1982-86

Architect:
Tadao Ando Architect & Associates
5-23, 2-Chome
Toyosaki, Kita-Ku
Osaka 531
Japan
Design Team:
Tadao Ando
Masataka Yano
Client:
Hirotaka and Hiroko Kidosaki
Structural Engineer:
Ascoral Architectural Structural
Engineering Co., Ltd

Villa Maesen
Zedelgem, Belgium
1989-92

Architect:
Stéphane Beel
Koningin Astridlaan 7/9
8200 Brugge
Belgium
Design Team:
Stéphane Beel
Hans Lust
Paul Van Eygen
Hans Verstuyft
Harm Wassink
Structural Engineer:
S C E S Brugge
Technical Engineer:
R Boydens Brugge

Beach house
Bermagui, NSW, Australia
1989-90

Architect:
Daryl Jackson
Daryl Jackson Pty Ltd
35 Little Bourke Street
Melbourne 3000
Victoria
Australia
Client:
Daryl and Kay Jackson
Structural Engineer:

Dale Simson,
Perrett Simpson Pty Ltd
Contractor:
Julian Barlow

The Eagle
Braunschweig, Germany
1989-92

Architect:
Dirk Alten Architects
Johannisberger Str.30
14197 Berlin
Germany
Design Team:
Dirk Alten
Client:
Heinz Alten
Structural Engineer:
Gerber und Tapppert
Main Contractor:
Otto Wrehde KG
Photograhy:
Ortwin Heipe

Cubist house
Yamaguchi, Japan
1990

Architect:
Shinichi Ogawa Atelier
401 1-11-25 Inokuchidai Nishi-ku
Hiroshima 733
Japan
Design Team:
Shinichi Ogawa
Tetsuya Tsukada
Tomoo Toba
Hiroshi Sanbuichi
Client:
Joji Nomura
Structural Engineer:
Uesugi Structural Engineers
General Contractors:
Shimada Corporation

Villa dall'Ava
St Cloud, Paris, France
1984-91

Architect:
Office of Metropolitan
Architecture
Boompjes 55, Rotterdam, 3011XB
The Netherlands
Design Team:
Rem Koolhaas
Xaveer de Geyter
Jeroen Thomas
Landscape Architect:
Yves Brunier
Site Supervisor:
Loïc Richalet
Interior Consultant:
Petra Blaisse
Structural Engineer:
Marc Mimram
General Contractor:
Entreprise Mare

The Monument
Joshua Tree, California, USA
1988-90

Architect:
Schweitzer BIM
5499 W. Washington Blvd
Los Angeles
CA 90016
USA
Design Team:
Josh Schweitzer
Meriwether Felt

Patrick Ousey
Scott Prentice
Eric Wendt
Clients:
Josh Schweitzer
Mary Sue Milliken
Susan Feniger
Barbara McReynolds
Gai Gherardi
Rhonda Saboff
Structural Engineer:
David-Fejes Engineers
Mechanical Engineer:
Comeau Engineers
Contractor:
Silverstrand Partnership

Cowes house
Phillip Island, Victoria, Australia
1984-94

Architect:
Denton Corker Marshall
49 Exhibition Street
Melbourne
Australia
Design Team:
Barrie Marshall
Client:
Barrie Marshall
Landscape:
Denton Corker Marshall
Structural Engineer:
Ove Arup & Partners
Contractor:
Rod Needham,
Loxlee Constructions

Winton guest house
Wayzata, Minnesota, USA
1983-87

Architect:
Frank O Gehry & Associates
1520 B Cloverfield Boulevard
Santa Monica
CA 90404
USA
Design Team:
Frank Gehry
Robert G Hale
John Clagett
C Gregory Walsh
Adolph Ortega
Mitch Lawrence
Carroll Stockard
Associate Architects:
Jeffrey Scherer
John Cook
Meyer, Scherer, Rockcastle
Client:
Mr and Mrs David M Winton
Structural Engineer:
Kurily & Szymanski
Contractor:
Joe Boyer & Sons, Inc

Zero Cosmology
Kagoshima, Kyushu, Japan
1989-91

Architect:
Masaharu Takasaki
1-14-32-402 Jingumae Shibuyaku
Tokyo
Japan
Design Team:
Masaharu Takasaki Architects
Client:
Uemura
Structural Engineer:
Yasuo Tanaka
Constructor:
Haruzono Gumi

La Casa del Ojo de Agua
Santiago Tepetlapa, Mexico
1985-90

Architect:
Ada Dewes and Sergio Puente
Architects
Carmen 34
Col. San Bernabé Ocotopec
Mexico 10300
Mexico
Design Team:
Ada Dewes and Sergio Puente
Client:
Ada Dewes and Sergio Puente
Structural Engineer:
Enrique Arriaga Architect

Price house
Corona del Mar, California, USA
1984-89

Architect:
Bart Prince Architect
3501 Monte Vista N.E
Albuquerque
New Mexico 87106
USA
Design Team:
Bart Prince – Design
Bill Kleinschmidt –
Working Drawings
Client:
Joe and Etsuko Price
Structural Engineer:
August Mosimann
Contractor:
Owner with Architect as Project
Manager
Project Foreman:
Eric Johnson

Casa Bianda
Losone, Ticino, Switzerland
1987-89

Architect:
Mario Botta Architetto
Via Ciani 16
6904 Lugano
Switzerland
Design Team:
Mario Botta
Work Directions:
Ennio Maggetti
Client:
Roberta and Gabriele Bianda
Structural Engineer:
Ing. Bonalumi

House in Brasschaat
Antwerp, Belgium
1990-93

Architect:
Xaveer de Geyter Architect
Kipdorp 21
B-2000 Antwerp
Belgium
Design Team:
Xaveer de Geyter
with Piet Crevits
Alain de Backer
Landscape Architect:
Yves Brunier
Structural Engineer:
Jeroen Thomas
Contractor:
Constant Goedleven N V

St Andrews house
Mornington Peninsula, Victoria,
Australia

1991
Architect:
Katsalidis Architects
171 Latrobe Street
Melbourne
Victoria 3000
Australia
Design Team:
Nonda Katsalidis
Nigel Fitton
Jaqui Wagner
Client:
Nonda Katsalidis
Structural Engineer:
Richard Eckhaus and Partners

Chmar house
Atlanta, Georgia, USA
1989

Architect:
Scogin Elam and Bray Architects
Inc.
Design Team:
Mack Scogin
Merrill Elam
Lloyd Bray
with Susan Desko
Structural Engineer:
Pruitt Eberly Inc
General Contractor:
Weleh Tarkington, Inc
Model Photography:
Lloyd Bray
Computer Photography:
Susan Desko

Casa Garau-Agusti
Belaterra, Barcelona, Spain
1988-93

Architect:
Enric Miralles Architect
52 Avinyó Str
08002 Barcelona
Spain
Design Team:
Enric Miralles
with Carmen Pinós
Client:
Garau-Agusti family
Structural Engineer:
BOMA
Collaborators:
Eva Prats

Truss Wall house
Tsurukawa, Machida-City, Japan
1991-93

Architect:
Ushida Findlay Partnership
402, 3-12-15, Kitashinagawa
Shinagawa-ku
Tokyo 141
Japan
Design Team:
Eisaku Ushida
Kathryn Findlay
Makoto Haseda
Tony Manzo
Hirofumi Tsuchiya
Client:
Truss Wall Company
Structural Engineer:
Yasuo Tanaka
Contractor:
Truss Wall Company & S S Projects

House with Studio
Kralingse, Rotterdam, The
Netherlands
1989-91

Architect:
Mecanoo architekten
Oude Delft 203
2611 HD Delft
The Netherlands
Design Team:
Erick van Egeraat
Francine Houben
with Theo Kupers
Bjarne Mastenbroek
Cock Peterse
Inma Fernandez-Pufg
Birgit Jügenhake
Marjolijn Adriaansche
Structural Engineer:
A B T adviesburo voor
bouwtechnick B V
Contractor:
Van Omme & de Groot B V

42 and 44 Rochester Place
Camden Town, London, UK
1977 and 1989

Architect:
David Wild Architect
44 Rochester Place
London NW1 9JX
44 Rochester Place:
Design Team:
David Wild
Client:
David Wild
Construction:
David Wild
Mark Wild
Ken Crawford
Structural Engineer:
John Romer
42 Rochester Place:
Design Team:
David Wild
Client:
Dan Tindall
Construction:
David Wild
Neil Manley
Ken Crawford
Andrew Crawford
Andrew Brooke
Ian Fairweather
Louise James
Mark Goldspink
Mark Wild
Structural Engineer:
John Romer

Haus im Vordertaunus
Wiesbaden, Germany
1989-92

Architect:
Studio Granda
Fjölnisvegi 2
IS-101 Reykjavík
Iceland
Competition Initiator & Organizer:
Galerie ZB Frankfurt
Design Team:
Margrét Hardardóttir
Steve Christer
Lárus Gudmunsson
Steinar Sigurdsson
with Ásdís Ágústsdóttir
Sólveig Berg Björnsdóttir
Associate Architects:
Planungsring Ressel & Partner
Model Maker:
Colin Hart
Landscape Architects:
Marten & Porlein
Gramenz
Structural Engineers:
Línuhönnun

Associate Structural Engineers:
Horst Schäfer
Contractors:
Concreteworks:
Brömer u Sohn
Cedar cladding, windows,
carpentry:
Holzbau Wagner
Aluminium windows:
Moba Fenster Aluminiunbau
Steelwork:
Müller Metallbau

Ken Done house
Mosman, NSW, Australia
1988-91

Architect:
Glenn Murcutt and Associates Pty
Ltd
176A Raglan Street
Mosman NSW
2088 Australia
Design Team:
Glenn Murcutt
with Reginald Lark
Client:
Ken and Judy Done
Landscape Architect:
Hosking Munro
Structural Engineer:
James Taylor and Associates Pty
Ltd.
Contractor:
Berg Brothers P/L

Yatsuka residence
Komae, Tokyo, Japan
1987-88

Architect:
Urban Project Machine
5-56-10-401 Matsubara
Setagaya-Ku
Tokyo
Japan
Design Team:
Hajime Yatsuka
Atsushi Maeda
Kyoko Nakazato
Client:
Hajime Yatsuka
Structural Engineer:
Hidehiro Iwamoto
Contractor:
Kudo Construction Company
Table Design:
Kenji Oki

Oakyard
The Keep, Blackheath, London,
UK
1991-93

Architect:
Allies and Morrison Architects
42 Newman Street
London W1P 3PA
Design Team:
Graham Morrison
Bob Allies
Joanna Green
Honor Thomson
Laurie Hallows
Deborah Miller
Structural Engineer:
Desmond Mairs, Whitby and Bird
Quantity Surveyor:
Colin Matley, Davis Langdon and
Everest
Contractor:
Stephen Boyle, Boyle Contracts

Index

Acknowledgements

The publishers and author are grateful to the following for providing illustrations for this book:
[t = top, b = bottom, c = centre, l = left, r = right]

Allies and Morrison Architects: 234tr, 235

Dirk Alten Architects: 93

John Amarantides/Frank Lloyd Wright Foundation: 109b

Tadao Ando Architect & Associates: 3, 64-5, 66c, 66b, 67, 71

© Wayne Andrews Esto: 17

Architectural Review: 10, 12t, 12b, 13, 24-25, 27, 72, 109t, 214, 234t, 10

Bauhaus Archive: 73

Stéphane Beel: 74t, 79t, 82, 83

Reiner Blunk: 121, 122-123, 125t, 126t, 126c, 126b, 127, 222, 223, 224b, 227b

Mario Botta Architect: 158r, 160, 161

Richard Bryant/Arcaid: 28, 29, 30tl, 30tr, 30bl, 32-33, 35t, 35b, 144t, 144b, 145, 146cr, 146b, 206, 207, 208, 210, 211t, 211b, 212t, 212b, 213, 215b

Alberto Campo Baeza Architect: cover, 56t, 56b, 57, 58-9, 60t, 60b, 61t, 61b, 62, 63

Peter Cook: 232, 233, 234b

Couturier/Archipress: 194-5

William J. R. Curtis: 26l, 26r

Denton Corker Marshall: 124, 125b 127t

Ada Dewes & Sergio Puente Architects: 146tr, 146tl, 147

Alberto Flammer: 158l

Frank O. Gehry & Associates: 132

Xaveer de Geyter Architect: 167

John Gollings Photography: 168-9, 170t, 170-71, 171t, 172, 174b

Ortwin Heipe: 90, 91, 92

Lucien Hervé: 196-97

Hiroyuki Hirai: 190l

Wolfgang Hoyt /© Esto: 38br

Timothy Hursley: 48-49, 50t, 51t, 51c, 51b, 52, 52-3, 54t, 54-5, 112-113, 114-115, 115r, 116, 117, 118l, 176t, 176cl, 177, 178, 179t, 180t, 180b, 180-181

Arata Isozaki & Associates: 98b

Daryl Jackson Pty Ltd: 84, 84-85, 86t, 86c, 86b, 87, 88, 89t, 89b

Katsalidis Architects: 173t, 173b,174t, 175

Katsuhisha Kida: 189r, 190t, 191t, 192b

Klaus Kinold: 80tl

Kenji Kobayashi: 188-9, 191b

Landesbildstelle Berlin: 76

Jannes Linders: 80tr

Mitsuo Matsuoka: 66t, 68t, 68b, 69, 70

Duccio Malagamba: 184, 185t, 185b

Mecanoo architekten: 200-201, 205b

Richard Meier & Partners: 42, 43

Norbert Miguletz: 199, 216-217, 218, 219t, 219b, 221r, 221l

Enric Miralles Architect: 185br, 186t, 186cl, 187,

Alan Morris: 198

Grant Mudford: 128-9, 130l, 130-131, 133, 134t, 134b, 135

Glenn Murcutt and Associates Pty Ltd: 225, 226, 227t

Pino Musi: 156, 157, 158-9

Office of Metropolitan Architecture: 102-103b, 103t, 104t, 105t

Shinichi Ogawa Atelier: 98t, 99

Oki Doki: 224tr, 224tl

Martin Pawley: 18

Pawson Silvestrin: 31, 34-35c

Alberto Emanuele Piovano: 78t, 78b, 79, 80b, 80-81

Antoine Predock Architect: 55

Bart Prince Architect: 111, 151tc, 151tr, 154

Robert Reck: 50b

© Hans Sautter/Colorific: 4, 110t, 136, 137, 138b, 139, 140-141, 141t, 141b, 142l

Scagliola/Brakkee: 202, 203t, 203b, 204, 205t

Scogin Elam and Bray Architects Inc: 179c, 179b, 182, 183

Schweitzer BIM: 118tr, 119

Shinkenchiku-sha: 94, 95, 96, 96-97

Julius Shulman: 11

Eric Sierins: 21

Filippo Simonetti: 44t, 44b, 45, 47tl, 47c, 47r

Luigi Snozzi Architect: 46

Stichting Beeldrecht, Amsterdam: 105

Ezra Stoller © Esto: 38bl

Tim Street-Porter: 6-7, 36-37, 38cl, 38tr, 39, 40-41, 41, 106, 130tr,

Studio Granda: 220

Masaharu Takasaki: 138t, 142rt-b, 143

Ushida Findlay Partnership: 192t, 193

Alan Weintraub: 148t, 148b, 149, 150, 152-3, 155t, 155bl, 155br

Hans Werleman: 100-101, 101r, 102, 104, 162-3, 164-5, 165r, 166

David Wild Architect: 208c, 208b, 209, 214tl, 214tr, 215t

Hajime Yatsuka: 228, 228-9, 229t, 230t, 230b, 231t

Alo Zanetta: 159r

Thanks:

Special thanks to Paul Finch, David Dunster, Tom Heneghan, Haig Beck, Jackie Cooper, Abby Bussell, Matthias Sauerbruch, Rik Nijs, Michael MacAulay, Peter Buchanan, Fumio Shimizu, Naoko Aono, Joachim Goetz, Franziska Heindl, Adrian Fitzgerald, Daryl Jackson, Francoise Arnold and Mikko Heikkinen for their ideas and suggestions.
And finally, and most importantly, to Douglas Peberdy for his toleration of my word processor over so many years.